ALSO BY JAY CANTOR

The Space Between: Literature and Politics
The Death of Che Guevara
Krazy Kat

ON GIVING BIRTH TO ONE'S OWN MOTHER

JAY CANTOR ON GIVING BIRTH TO ONE'S OWN MOTHER ESSAYS ON ART AND SOCIETY

 ALFRED A. KNOPF   NEW YORK   1991

THIS IS A BORZOI BOOK
PUBLISHED BY ALFRED A. KNOPF, INC.

Most of the essays from this work were originally published
in *California* magazine, *Conjunctions, Southwest Review, Tikkun,
TriQuarterly,* and *The Yale Review.*
The author would like to thank the Guggenheim Foundation
for its support during the writing of this book.

Library of Congress Cataloging-in-Publication Data
Cantor, Jay.
On giving birth to one's own mother: essays on art and society /
by Jay Cantor. — 1st ed.
p.   cm.
ISBN 0-394-58752-9
1. Arts and society.   2. Popular culture.   I. Title.
NX180.S6C36   1991
700'. 1'03—dc20   90-52948

Manufactured in the United States of America
First Edition

With love, for

ELEANOR WESCHLER CANTOR,

*who so skillfully imagined me first,
and then, kindly and carefully,
did the necessary early revisions*

CONTENTS

ON GIVING BIRTH TO ONE'S OWN MOTHER

THE PATRIARCHS

I. MODERN DISASTERS/POST-MODERN DESPAIR

☐   The New Man—those words, spoken in this century by
so many tyrants, martyrs, and dreamers, by Mao, by Che
Guevara, by Futurist artists and surrealist poets, by all who
wished to announce that a new heaven and a new earth would
require and produce a new humanity—those words now cast
an ominous shadow on the names of Marx, and Nietzsche, and
Freud, the patriarchs of the tribes of the modern. It has often
seemed to me, these last fifteen years or so, as if the dispensa-
tions given by these patriarchs—and they were *patriarchal*
indeed—their interrogations, and their projects for our redemption, had ended, chilled by that shadow. For many, of
course, the modern epoch, as these men apprehended it, had
concluded—or they wished it had—earlier than a mere fifteen
years ago. Yet I still wonder how we can work through our
bewilderments outside of their themes.

No, conservatives would say, the question should be, how
are we going to repair the damage the patriarchs' ideas have
done? By studying Socrates, says one. By dismantling the

overweening state, says another. By intoning the pledge of allegiance, or repeating the words "family values." But simply to wish that the modern project, as these men each inflected it, was over, having ended in failure or tyranny, means, usually, that one's thinking comes not truly after the patriarchs' questions but as if one had lived before they needed to be asked. The conservative philosophers and politicians have not really replied to, but rather repressed or ignored, the questions these men still pose.

Humanity, the patriarchs said, in the absence (or silence) of God, makes itself, even at the most basic of levels; and—though each would put our hands on a different lever—each thought that we must remake ourselves to meet the challenge of our new possibilities for productive work and for self-destruction, to fulfill (or, in Nietzsche's case, truly to overcome) our need for connectedness, for satisfying community. Perhaps only such a new community (or an "overman") might intertwine eros with death so that life might continue.

And despite the current euphoria that we are history's happy culmination, I think we still need the patriarchs' projects and their insights. The peoples of Eastern Europe move towards systems, like liberal capitalism, that promise them a greater say in their own making. But that hardly means that in the prosperous West we can't imagine for ourselves a fuller democracy, a greater participation in shaping *our* history. We will confront then the question of what our relative prosperity is *for*, how we *wish* to form ourselves. Addressing that question in the Sixties, America produced examples of exuberant if flawed generosity in the war on poverty, and an efflorescence of experimental lives (many of the experiments failed, many of the lives were wasted). But America decided, as the world recurrently has, to spend itself most fully on war. Could the patriarchs' ideas lead to a more profound sense of what would bring us a vivid life in their teachings that our most difficult but most satisfying activity would be to participate fully (socially and individually) in our self-creation? Could the patriarchs' questions lead us to an ever greater comprehension of the myriad forces that make us, and to a larger say in that making?

For in any case, we are made and remade. Even now— willy-nilly—our nervous systems are newly extended by computer networks; and, by gene splicing, humanity physically reshapes itself. So the patriarchs' questions continue to trouble me: *Can we direct our remaking?* Should this remaking be left to the hidden hand of the marketplace—supposing there *is* such a hidden hand, that the market's many greedy fingers aren't impelled by advertising, by already existing power? Couldn't that power truly be democratically dispersed? Or made wise (so ask Freud and Nietzsche) in some other, nobler way?

Or should we be satisfied by the piecemeal workings of the entrepreneurial imagination? Responding to any demand for an active social imagination—whether thought of as a community activity, or as the work of solitary makers—the market instead offers "lifestyles" to purchase, a kitful of products along with narratives which give the goods glamour and meaning. The market's "lifestyle" pleasures are mostly matters of product design and engineered consent—the pleasures not of deep innovation or activity but of contemplative aesthetics, of looking admiringly at the design of one's life (one's lifestyle), as if it were a series of pictures in a glossy magazine. Discussing a fantasy styled by advertisers substitutes for the imaginative work, the communal conversation, that makes foundational metaphors for a society. To be in fashion together is our new community and our remaking—not the new humanity, but the new suits and dresses. Yet the fashion fantasies are not transformative; in peasant blouses we aren't peasants; in Fifties gear, we are not our parents. Restlessly, we change partners, change clothes.

Do we even care? Or perhaps we think that to search out transformative communal fantasies, rich with our hidden desires, will only make matters worse. A passivity before the great god of fashion, the god *that which happens,* gives an air at once desperate and enervated to much contemporary painting or narrative or critique. This feeling, of an old dispensation ended, of an interregnum time (but without hope of the new) is often the weather of the "post-modern." Post-modernism sometimes seems a historical term, and sometimes a trademark; what *I* mean by it here is a despairing irony towards the modern projects, but—and delineating flavors of irony is a crucial post-modern botany, for some ironies strengthen, and some poison—a fairly comfortable condo-ized despair. "In the real dark night of the soul," F. Scott Fitzgerald wrote, "it is always three o'clock in the morning." Three o'clock, Scott? Time for late night T.V.! ("Are we having fun yet?") There is, said former President Carter, a malaise in the land. We listened, and changed; changed the channel, anyway. But perhaps he was right. And I don't think the malaise has passed with our new prosperity.

I try to remember what channel we were on when the malaise began. Was it, for me, in 1975, when the United States left Vietnam—Operation Eagle Pull—our diplomats and their families rising from the Embassy roof, with Vietnamese holding on to the struts of the helicopters. The North Vietnamese Army advanced and a wave of refugees poured in front of them, fleeing—but from where to where? In Cambodia, the

Khmer Rouge, furious, insane, silent, took over Phnom Penh, cleared the city, even the hospital rooms, made the inhabitants march to their death in the countryside. The patriarchs' theories, which so many intellectuals had imagined would account for our history and guide our re-creation of our selves and our world, were, it began to seem, unlivable, tyrannical, paltry, inadequate, deceptive, and, finally, terrifying.

That I remain attached to the patriarchs' projects may mark me as from the "Sixties"—part vintage, part brand-name— member of a generation whose ideas and actions had a great deal about them of a costume show (that is, we sometimes acted as if the Administration Building was the Czar's Winter Palace), of the grandiose (at worst we thought the whole world was watching, was about to join us; at best we thought we were about to join the world); of the misguided; perhaps even, critics say, of the duplicitous. Was the movement self-deceived from the first? Did we want the war in Vietnam over, or just the draft that threatened us? Myself, I think there is no question that Allan Bloom, for example, in his almost hysterical critique of that decade, is wrong: We wanted the war over. In fact the Sixties were, for most people working against the Vietnam War, a time of dark, often inappropriate but very palpable guilt. Perhaps the anti-war activists were not as willing to be tried on conspiracy charges, jailed, beaten, or killed as their critics now wish they had been—if they were to show *proper* seriousness. And compared, of course, to the history of the union movement or the civil rights movement, and most certainly in comparison to the violence of the war itself, those dangers were, in fact, slight. But a good part of what caused the movement against the Vietnam War, and the broader movement for justice of which it was a part, to trickle to an end was not simply that our self-interest had been met with the end of the draft, or that (as was indeed the case) our vision of justice—of a world remade—was often muddy and not about to convince our fellow citizens. In addition, we were afraid of the force we faced and the kinds of violence (legal and otherwise) that it might unleash; and we were all too easily bewildered by the state's many efforts to confuse the left—to infiltrate and subvert and incite us to stupid and destructive actions. Terrified, we often rended one another. We were anxious soldiers, indeed—and afraid, in my case, of *any* outcome, for the complicated, riven city was the air I had been formed by and loved; and perhaps in the struggle as I imagined it, between first world (as city) and third world (as countryside), I lost either way.

But there was moral feeling as well as moralism in our actions, compassion as well as disguised ambition in the people I knew who worked to end the war. And there was, too, a sense that ordinary social life could be—and, given the world's new resources of violence, must be—very different from what we had experienced (in an admittedly limited way) before. There was, in our marches, moratoriums, sit-ins, poster-making, leafletting, a taste of shared enterprises, of trying to make sense of the world for the first time—new to us Mirandas!—of grasping, at least intellectually, the forces that made us; there was a taste of conviviality, and community. Bloom, in his *The Closing of the American Mind,* his own mind haunted to the point of closure by irresponsible black students at Cornell foolishly, dangerously, holding rifles, remembers this as a defiantly and disgustingly anti-intellectual time. He was not, of course, alone in this. During the strike at Harvard in 1969, several fine professors slept in the stacks of Widener Library to protect the books from the specter of violent students. But those students were ghosts indeed, for my own experience as a student, and (I've found since I became a professor) that of many colleagues now who were teaching then, was directly contrary to Bloom's. We were desperate (perhaps, indeed, too desperate) for knowledge, for understanding. Whatever of value we learned was constantly on our lips, to be shared, argued about (which may have made us sometimes obstreperous in the classroom), and rethought, as we tried to make the knowledge help us in what seemed like terrible predicaments. We had been born into a world capable of holocausts of efficient mechanized savagery, Nazi assembly lines of death, a time capable of ending time in a nuclear flash-boom, an economy engaged in prodigies of sublime space flight, of distance-annihilating communication; we were citizens of a nation with the abundance, privileges, and horrors of empire. Yet it seemed that we lacked the political imagination to re-form ourselves and our polity to control our new possibilities for connection, or our new resources of violence— resources that might better shape the world, or destroy others, or cause us to die ourselves. We lacked, sometimes, even the concepts to acknowledge our situation. Our intellectual heroes, like Herbert Marcuse, or my own teacher, Norman O. Brown, were, Bloom feels, misguided choices, and Bloom is indeed caustic in his contempt towards these and others of his intellectual superiors, artists and writers like Mary McCarthy, or Louis Armstrong. These ill-chosen targets are, as he says, stand-ins for the real villains, Marx, and Freud, and Nietzsche. (The Americans, sloppy scholars, got it wrong, misunderstood their Nietzsche. How much worse, though, from Bloom's point of view, if they had gotten it right! I feel in Bloom's almost fetishistic repetition of certain admired names that he knows that Nietzsche's description of our problems is more powerful than his own prescription for them. Thus the considerable and unpleasant irritability of his book, and its sometimes quite moving pathos.) In any case, there were intellectual heroes in the Sixties, like Brown and Marcuse, Fanon, Simone de Beauvoir, John Coltrane, Jean-Luc Godard, Buckminster Fuller, Bob Dylan, Allen Ginsberg, Grace Paley, Thomas Pynchon, authors of complicated, insightful, demanding theoretical works and songs and films and stories, helpful in what seemed (and still seems to me) our necessary project of self-understanding and communal transformation.

I remember that time, too, as a sleepless, brooding, anxious period—one must not be, in the words we inappropriately, hyperbolically used at the time, "a good German." That guilt towards the war's victims—Vietnamese and Americans—no doubt clouded our vision, and distorted our action. One felt guilty towards the Vietnamese, and towards the mostly working-class Americans who were fighting the war on behalf of . . . well, here opinions differed. Whose war was it? A mistake by the foreign policy community, the best and the brightest? A piece of imperial geopolitics; a move against the Soviets or the Chinese? Part of what we desperately wanted for our project was the answer to those questions, so that our nation might not make this mistake—and was it a *mistake*?—again. Vietnam seemed not truly a war *for* the Vietnamese, but against them. And a war whose heaviest price was paid by the Vietnamese and by the American working class. A duplicitous rewriting of this time, and of the movement against the war, has already occurred, so that harder questions of what created the war needn't be answered. Instead, ever-present class resentments are used to create a tasty, emotionally satisfying version of our defeat: The privileged, middle-class, anti-war protesters are remembered as savage towards the working-class American soldiers, holding them guilty of war crimes, destroying their morale. (There is an honest rendering of the sour stew of emotions that such deception feeds on in John Updike's reminiscences of his feelings during the Sixties, an essay in his book *Self-Consciousness.*) In fact, few movement people who were involved in thinking through the causes of the war were so insane as to think that the *soldiers* were the cause; they knew that the soldiers acted, usually honorably, often heroically, within a larger madness that they had not created, but which might make them and their comrades victims.

For some, the tragi-comical, grandiose, and overblown aspects of our actions against the war—our songs, our profanity, our costume show, even our Yippie nihilism—discredit the movement. Our foolish, theatrical irony is easily lampooned by writers like Bloom. We were Cagney, shouting "Top of the world, Ma!" in *White Heat*—not an actual gangster, but Cagney. We lacked, according to Bloom, the "European" seriousness of "true" nihilism. Perhaps whatever else our actions were, they were *also* always comical, and that in itself I don't find regrettable or intellectually dishonest. Bloom misses much of what's vital in American culture, including the particular sort of American irony that allows Americans to mean very seriously what's jokingly said. That antic quality often, it seems to me, opened into a different idea of what political action and community should feel like. Perhaps it was of a piece, too, with our youth, and the slight level of risk we ran in this prosperous and usually forgiving country. Our community was, in part, "Hey Judy, I've got a barn, let's put on a show!" partaking of that deceptive, charmingly vulgar Hollywood sweetness, that tingly feeling of being onstage. We were a Pepsi Generation—or, in Jean-Luc Godard's phrase, "the children of Marx and Coca-Cola"—of ideology and television and film, an image-irradiated group of people. No wonder we saw ourselves first of all in terms provided for us by the mass culture that had, from childhood on, helped make us up. No wonder, too, that as the war dragged on, we distorted ourselves in order to have our anti-war show renewed by the T.V. news, so that we could make other people up.

But that double-vision of ourselves, that we were "playing," using provocative "costumes" and chants, like numbers in a musical comedy, that vision was ours as well as our critics', and gave one an empowering self-mockery (another flavor of irony!) that can come from seeing oneself in the guise of figures from popular culture. It's a very American ability. (Are we Americans drawn to stage our lives because we want to differentiate ourselves from the masses, the audience, in our mass culture? Or is it our road-show production of "a nation of prophets," where sometimes you're the performer, sometimes I am? Or is it because we are so saturated by the media that the stage sometimes seems the only space we have in common?)

But there are brief moments when the stage is only as big as the street corner, a moment when the style, usually from some part of the nation (usually the African-American leavening) that isn't yet fully written on by the productive machinery, throws up some fragment of a rhythmical, articulated, bold walk, produces a fresh harmony in street-corner singing, a new style of dancing, a new way of staging some aspect of life. For a moment that production lies outside the corporate orbit—though now the corporation moves rapidly, and, as the ads quickly enough said in the late nineteen-sixties, "the spirit of the revolution is on Columbia Records." Still, the Sixties were, however briefly, a time when those fragments of style—

which were just in the process of distorting themselves to get a "wider audience"—seemed to coalesce for a moment into a "youth culture," a time when the staged quality of American life embodied, as it recurrently does, an independent American spirit.

That doubled quality (that one is oneself, yet playing a role in the community's small-scale production, a play which demands certain lines from you, which makes you up) was hardly original to the Sixties; it's part of what often makes events in the United States seem so funny to the rest of the world, even when we are, far more truly than in the Sixties, revolutionizing ourselves. (In fact, that sly wink, like Cary Grant giving Archie Leach as his alias in *His Girl Friday,* is part of what has made our movies themselves so appealing.) Americans' ability to be onstage and backstage (or in the audience—for sometimes, at our democratic best we almost eliminate the difference), and so laugh at our self-importance, has always been part of what has so far freed America from European extremities (like the desperate nihilism Allan Bloom rightly fears). It marks one difference between Leni Riefenstahl's *Triumph of the Will,* and Busby Berkeley's *Footlight Parade.* For in each film large assemblages synchronize to form the image of their leader. In Riefenstahl, the Nuremberg rally participants embody in their combination of frenzy and rigidity the dictator's will; their groupings are sentences from his mouth. In Berkeley, each dancer holds a piece of a photo. Together they make a giant composite picture of FDR. Then, at the conclusion of the film, we focus in on a little flip-book in Cagney's hand. As he twirls the pages, a ship moves away from us, the lovers no doubt on board. A flipbook, to take us backstage, to say, see, this is how motion is made, it's a trick on the eye. That saving distance, the ability to be backstage, gave America its special sense of itself as, during the Thirties and Forties, it reshaped the American compact; it provided our uncynical American irony, and allowed for the dance.

But this once-saving irony—that you can understand that it's all a show, while still participating—has itself become part of the American spectacle in a way that even Busby Berkeley couldn't have foreseen. Now we're not playful, ironic actors, each holding our fragment of the president's photo, jointly producing his image; instead our post-modern irony produces a new combination of roles: spectator, and enervated, passive director. That sense that one is backstage, like a director, is another way that one is now made to feel "special," different from the rubes who don't understand how they're manipulated. But we're still manipulated. We didn't even have to see through the way the candidates fooled us in the presidential election just past. The T.V. commentators did the seeing through for us, made taking us backstage a part of the spectacle, told us how "spin doctors" worked to influence the reporting, analyzed the psychic buttons pushed by the candidates' television commercials. One became, then, an ironic voter—an individual supposedly different from the mass, by virtue of the seeing through that the mass media themselves provided. A new species of Nietzscheanism was born: Yes, we see that there is only aesthetics, only lies, and so we consciously value the most artful lie—even the lie, perhaps, that we are somehow different from the masses because of our aesthetic appreciation of lies! Hey, why kick—that's show biz! that's entertainment! Yet the buttons were still pushed, and the levers eventually pulled.

The winking gaiety of the Sixties seems a different variety of irony, one that was still part of a show that we (barely,

barely) made rather than simply watched. Our sense of experimentation, the sense, very American indeed, of *possibility* and play seemed precious to me at the time. But now the dangers press into memory as well. Possibility for what? (Even the patients dragging their I.V.'s were forced to leave Phnom Penh. To die on the road as part of the Khmer Rouge's mass murder.) And again a different sort of irony seeps through, the post-modern despair. Why *not* just lean back in one's seat, and enjoy the entertainment—if you try to participate in history, to change the world, you'll only make matters worse! It is, I think, the wreck of our "Sixties" hopes, our "modern" project for transformation, and the ensuing distrust of ourselves, that has given rise to much of the current post-modern irony. We are afraid now of both our instructive ecstasies and our foolish excess, and uncertain anymore that we can tell the difference. We can't quite surrender our memory of the sometimes terrifying pleasures of the Sixties, the near unhingement that can come from the sense of a world and a self that can be remade. Yet we're unable to shoulder the task again; uncertain, even, if we should. All this forms itself into uneasy amalgams of self-dislike, and icy angry contempt, of cynicism (hey, I'm no rube!), and nostalgia.

But strolling through the mall, in an almost dazed happiness indistinguishable from comfortable despair (are we having fun yet?), I find myself surprised by my own anger when others, in theory, in criticism, and in their artistic and political practice, join me in a mocking funeral of the patriarchs' projects. I find my fellow mourners' glee unnerving, their comments boorish or duplicitous. Often, it seems, it is not the inadequacy of the theories or the solutions proposed by these thinkers that the critics truly object to; rather, the burial party simply wishes the problem the patriarchs identified—the intolerable prison that history will become to us if it does not become the field of our making—ignored.

I still find, as I think most people do who directly confront these men, these texts, and their history in the world, something profound, complicated, and salutary in their attempts to go to the root of our unhappiness, something invigorating as well as frightening in their anger and their hopefulness, when, rightly or wrongly, they imagine a world and a self transformed. Their expectations, even the dour Freud's hopes, are, to our current taste, hyperbolic at best and menacing at worst. Is there a way to savor and be fed by that hopefulness without being misled into foolishness or tyranny? Did the collapse of their projects mean the finale, too, of the hopes they represented? Does the collapse of Marxism mean there is no human solidarity possible, little chance for a collective dialogue about our own making? That we can simply forget that our "self" is the product of a historical struggle that will, in any case, form and re-form us? Does Nietzsche's embrace by the fascists (and the aspects of his thought that made this death grip possible) mean that we must be suspicious of our possibilities for ecstatic action, for salutary tragedy? Does the sour careerism of the psychoanalytic profession mean that we cannot have (at the least) clear vision, or (at most, or at maddest) a transformed thought, a "reason of the heart," enriched at each moment by the symbolic dimension of our lives? Can we find a new language convivially to discuss our true needs? Can we feel a connection with nature that will encourage a less wasteful, less angry relation to the world that supports and co-creates us?

Even if one could overcome the ironic, post-modern ethos, one can't, of course, expect to discover oneself the new foundational metaphors for a society, the new apprehension of the transcendent values, or the transformed reason that we may need to discuss that project. But now I think our difficulty is even to remember the true dimensions of that need, remember accurately the frightening problems the patriarchs' own work has been implicated in, but remember also that we can't therefore turn away from the profound contradictions, and fresh possibilities, that they've revealed. A problem they have revealed is not, necessarily, a problem they created, and forgetting their work won't cause the difficulty to disappear.

To defeat my peevish irony I return to the years that mark my vintage, when I think that questions of social and self-remaking were intensely asked. I reread my past by the light of the patriarchs' ideas, and allow my past and its bewilderments to interrogate their works, so that, after the long sleep of the past decade, I can reknit my involvement with these texts and look for what they might still ask our present. The ways we now can hear these patriarchs challenging one another's answers, and, alas, listing one another's failures, may help us to sharpen the questions that confront us if we decide to take up their challenges. In this way we can at least hope to overcome a post-modern despair. That is to say, we can, at least, hope.

II. REREADING THE PAST

☐ The war in Vietnam was the event that bore down on my generation, twining into its awful majesty the more distant traumas of the atomic bomb, and the dark half-whispered story of the Holocaust (in part, the story that racism might end in genocide). Perhaps the way these previous blows were intertwined by Vietnam was unfortunate, each distorting the others (so that we sometimes confused the Vietnam War with genocide). But their combination also gave an added urgency to the several causes, formed them into one garment, helped weave them into the "Movement."

The war forced Marx's work on one's attention—even if one eventually rejected that work as not of our weather—because Marx was, ostensibly, the way the communist forces in Vietnam made sense of their world. If what one was told about the war by our leaders seemed false, perhaps the contrary view was the true one?

What one finds first in Marx—from the earliest *Economic and Philosophical Manuscripts of 1844* and on throughout his work—is a prescient critique of the rapacious individual that the capitalist economy creates, and of capitalism's formation, or deformation, of community, of politics, art, and morality, even of love. Marx's work is a prophet's outcry against our universal anti-value, money, whose corrosive power confounds all qualities, making the untalented seem talented (isn't "he who has power over the talented . . . more talented than the talented"?), the ugly seem beautiful ("I can buy the most *beautiful* of women for myself. Therefore I am not *ugly,* for the effect of *ugliness*—its power to repel—is nullified by money."), and the unlovable loved. Marx is describing the poisonous drug *as if:* For when the Lord of Capital looks at his "trophy wife," does he *really* feel attractive in her mirror-eyes, or does he feel it is *as if* she loved *him*? (And when the poison spreads inwardly, isn't it as if he feels that it is as if she loved him?) Soon it infects even our simpler lives, and we, too, may feel that it's *as if* the high-priced doctor *cares* for us, the professor lives to educate us, till mostly we may only know, and so come to accept, *as if* concern, *as if* love.

Marx, of course, overstates; his angry irony is often so broad as to be almost invisible, a nearly mechanical enumerative overkill. His prose attempts to match what he finds to be the prodigious, exploitative, daemonic energy of capitalism, its ability to dissolve the real, its calculating, quantifying power, which makes only what can be profitably counted, count. (Norman O. Brown, putting history on the analyst's couch, aptly diagnoses this as capitalism's "anal-obsessive character.") Marx's economic predictions may indeed be wrong, and the states which pretended, or still pretend, to think of themselves as founded on his principles (though there is little in his work that would describe how such a state should be organized or its economy managed) have been both tyrannical and unproductive. But for all its flaws, his critique, describing the many formative affiliations between the way we earn our livings and the selves and the lives we make, still has bite, especially as it has been elaborated and refined, with great sociological and philosophical sophistication, by such twentieth century Marxists as Gramsci, and Adorno, Horkheimer, Marcuse, and Guy Debord (whose gnomic, suggestive *Society of the Spectacle* has greatly helped me with the quandary of the nineteen-eighties). They have elucidated the exfoliations of the capitalist *attitude* in our consciousness, the way that economic life shapes our instincts, our ideas of pleasure (not satisfying work but distracting spectacles that overwhelm consciousness). And capitalism makes our fleeting moments of vivid impulse, of resistance and escape—our secret dream songs, our stammering rebellious chants—into spectacular, smooth films and slick records to be sold to us. Perhaps the critique, more than the dream of community, is what will be most lasting in Marx's work. But the fantasy of a society where there is a true and happy congruence—even an identity—between one's needs and the needs of one's society, where my comrades' development *enables* mine, this dream gives Marx's criticism of our world both a bitterness and acuity, as the Kingdom of Heaven does to Christianity's critique of this fallen world. Marx's heaven denies many of the solaces of our current civilization—after all, it is hard indeed to evoke love, and it may seem a comfort that one might buy it (or something like it). Instead Marx imagines for us a more profound pleasure and a purer pain (to confront that place where the contradictions of one's life are felt most deeply as what inevitably constitute one, that realm once called tragic): "Assume *man* to be *man,* and his relationship to the world to be a human one: then you can exchange love only for love, trust for trust . . . If . . . through a *living expression* of yourself as a loving person you do not make yourself a *loved person,* then your love is impotent and a misfortune." The tragic contradictions of our life pose us a question—but it is not how the contradictions might be resolved, rather it is how we might more fully embody them, achieve a more sublime reduction, a greater nakedness.

Marx's voice is prophetic; his work wields angry transcendental judgments, and a communion in which all differences are burned up. Like many prophetic visions, enthroned it is tyranny. Marx thought there was only one power that made us—the economic; his work doesn't imagine compelling competing centers of power by which we are also made, nor can it imagine a negotiation between these centers, those momentary alliances that make up the structure of our social life. (After all, love also requires difference.)

Perhaps the Marxist idea of society as communion—the near-fusion of each with each into one internationale—is impossible on this earth, for it may ignore a need for individual differences as part of any ego's construction, even if those differences are themselves only fantasies. Can we, even in our most utopian dreams, imagine that we could bear fully to overcome the ego, and its competitive self-overvaluing, except in brief moments of ecstatic fusion? In the name of communion, the communist state tried to root out all competing sources of power, all difference—except that between party and mass, leader and led—until one felt that earthly communion means tyranny. So it is difficult to remember that we may have an unfulfilled need for some profound joining, that it may be difficult for earthly life to continue *with* each ego so overvaluing its distinctions—what Freud calls "the narcissism of small differences"—each "I" insisting on its angry separation from the natural world and from others. Mustn't one have the sense that one is joined to a community that extends one's life, that the society (as well as one's own efforts) gives some shape to one's name, and so allows for continuity over generations? If our mark *on* the world (and how marked and marred it has become!) is made against that world, and by our own efforts only, the expression of our essence alone, then won't the world overcome it eventually, and write over us? Perhaps there is a question still posed us by Marx about how society can be combined with the onrush of technology so that we can have a say in our making.

The hero of Marx's drama, his march towards the community he imagined, was a necessarily revolutionary proletariat (necessarily: for without revolution, the workers would never have a sufficiency of the world's goods, or the world's freedom). Those who have only their labor to sell, the proletarians, struggle for control of their lives against the ruling bourgeoisie who own the means of production that *all* need to make their living. Like playwrights at an out-of-town tryout, this drama has often been revised by contemporary Marxists throughout the world. In order to gain followers or account for failures, thinkers of both the new and old left, here and abroad, have nervously put new actors in the old roles: A third world (meaning that part of the underdeveloped world instructed by communist forces and ideas) fights an international capitalist class, led by the United States, and represented by its military power. Sometimes the American working class was thought to be better off because of American interventions abroad; but eventually, many contemporary Marxists hoped, it would see that it, too, was exploited, that its freedom, too, lay in overthrowing the international bourgeoisie. And sometimes, as in the Sixties, the idea of a sufficiency of the world's goods was re-visioned to mean not goods to purchase, but an opportunity for creative activity, for leisure that was not filled with spectacles to distract us from work's pain, but leisure as a vast new realm, freedom as a majority of one's day. This reversal of proportions of work and leisure, would, Marxists like Herbert Marcuse thought, create men and women who were no longer tyrannized by the needs of production, a humanity inwardly and outwardly ready for satisfying, self-chosen projects, ones that were as wickedly frustrating and libidinally satisfying as the creation of art. Such activities of pleasant pain would fuse eros and death.

The appeal of Marxism in the Sixties, however the terms were manipulated, went beyond this vision of a nation of playful artists. Primarily, I think, it was this: Marxism was an apparently coherent theory that seemed to make sense of the world. Like paranoia, Marxism is capable of drawing all social details into its idea of an international conspiracy, the satanic equivalent of the heavenly internationale to come. Most especially Marxism gave words for a fundamental and, I think, still valid apprehension from the Sixties, that the Vietnam War was most troubling because its roots weren't delineated by the language of our everyday politics and morality. The patriarchs, each in their way, suggested forces in the collective or personal unconscious—imperialist exploitation, a neurotic death instinct, an unhinged, rancorous will (on all sides of the struggle)—that surpassed the unsatisfactory reasons our common discourse offered for the why of the war. Marx, like each of these men, claims far too much for his explanatory system. Marxism claims that the levers of the creation of the self, with all its appetites and its violence, lie in the form of life required by a certain kind of economic production—"the relations of production." For capitalism those relations are classes, and the sorts of personality and consciousness appropriate to each class. Of course, we can—following contemporary thinkers like Ernesto Laclau and Chantal Mouffe—correct Marx: We're made in part—or parts of us are made—by other means beside the economic (whose alliances with the economic make up the texture of our social life). And these alliances also make up our personality, for the self, too, is at each moment a unity of many elements. One is not just a worker, but a worker who is a father who is a Jew who is a patriot, and, in the collage that is the self, each of these elements modifies the meaning of the others. (Like Whitman, we each contain multitudes.) We can climb into the traditions that give meaning to these elements and change them if we must (finding a new meaning of Jew, for example, or of gender); and when we imagine a more democratic America, we will give these areas real standing along with the economic. Still, Marx has an important reminder to offer us: one important fragment of this collage is always made by the economic, by how we make our living. (What spirit, what force, forms the collage? Perhaps this will take us back to the principles of human solidarity; both without and within the annealing of the fragments requires love.)

So class can't account for all of one's significant decisions, for one's style as an artist or one's style as a lover, one's passion, one's jealousy. But does this mean, as that post-modern irony which I think was partially formed by the seeming destruction of Marxism would have it, that thought is always broken against the rocks of the actual? And then? Should one conclude, with a deconstructionist irony so skeptical about any positive statement that one shouldn't even call one's positions "conclusions," that no gain in our self-understanding is possible, that we can only register the inevitable defeat of understanding? A sense of the self as socially made—without hope that one can participate meaningfully in that making—leads to cynical irony. After reading Marx (and Nietzsche and Freud) we may think that there are no real haloes, no transcendent truths, no fixed self given by God and outside our communal making. Yet we find we can't have coherent lives without (for example) participating in patriotism, filial love, or the belief there are "callings" and caring that go beyond economic necessity. So even as the student (for example) speaks with apparent respect for the vocation of the revered teacher, he betrays in his gestures, his posture, his tone of voice, that he doesn't foolishly mean his reverence. He's wised-up and knows that the teacher's concern costs so much per hour, that the calling is also only a job. So we say and take back; irony that tastes like a sharp, bitter alkaloid becomes our daily drug, a substance we abuse to protect our self-respect as we suffer a fate that we do not make. Hey, we say by our irony, we're no rubes! But how, apart from actively rejoining the conflicts that form our shared values and our self, can we overcome our sense of impotence towards the world?

Throughout the century, Marxism has seemed to many a way to join the conflict that makes us, to join the largest struggle imaginable; it aligned one, if not with a force inevitably triumphant (though some certainly felt this), at least with a side in the struggle that was ostensibly for free development of human capacity and community. Were other sides possible that might more effectively, more truly, have brought about that free development? Most of us in the Sixties thought so; most did not look for examples or direction from communist states, and were, indeed, savagely critical of their demonic parodies of community. Yet we could give only the dimmest picture of that other force, that grand alliance of many different kinds of deeply felt oppression, something different from class alone—but including class among its elements—that we called "The Movement." In a struggle between a coherent institutionalized theory like Marxism, and a dimly felt intuition of another understanding, well, it's the rare Reformation when the established doctrine doesn't triumph—at least, for a time.

Through Marx, one could see one's actions as having important consequences, the Messiah's arrival depending on an action you might perform here; now. Class is a potent way to speak of that . . . moment . . . agglomeration . . . force, that is both within and without the personality, that place where one feels oneself, at very deep levels indeed, as being made by the social order. But class, as a force that forms one's politics, one's ideas, one's life, is an open secret easily forgotten in America. Or remembered in farcical versions, like *The Official Preppy Handbook,* with its pretense that we are discussing not power or privilege but taste in beer—a "lifestyle." America, perhaps more than any previous nation, fulfills its promise of mobility between classes, even if far less frequently than one might wish. So one often forgets class. Marx's class critique may only give a partial telling, but it gained additional force in many minds from how little place class had previously had in most Americans' thinking.

Of course there were aspects of the New Left's attraction to Marxism that were stuffed with illusion, not just an ignorance of history, but a cavalier euphoria towards it—for in the Sixties one thought, propelled by high-octane American optimism, that the "mistakes" of all previous revolutions, no matter how monstrous, could be avoided, that they were the far from inevitable consequences of those countries' underdevelopment. Was this optimism entirely mad? *Must* economic self-government, community and workplace democracy, inevitably turn into the Red Army and the Leninist Party? Perhaps now, as the long deformation of life in Eastern Europe comes to an end, new social imaginings may become possible, ones that make use of shards of insight from Marx, and avoid the horrifying Leninist outrages. Leninism, with its central and secret and absolute command structure, is a war machine, formed by the necessities of battle against absolutism. But those who control such war machines will of course always find new enemies—within if not without—to ensure that their rule remains necessary. Perhaps now, with the collapse of the Leninist war machinery, and with a possible diminution of our own, we, too, can rebegin the task of imagining the institutions that will make for greater democracy—each of us having a real vote in the decisions that shape our workplace or our environment, a substantial say in the structure of a society that will also, inevitably, partly structure each of us.

Of course many in the Sixties, as before, were drawn to Marxism by fantastical Leninist ambitions, fantasies of war, and a desire to be part of an imaginary central committee directing that war. Marx seemed to hand one the script to history—thus the horrifying certainty of the communist parties, or our American Leninist mini-groups, each claiming to be the "real" party. They thought they knew what sacrifices *must* be made, what ends would *inevitably* be served. And with the script in hand, one might be within history, acting, but somehow outside it. Backstage again, but this time in the director's chair, no longer an onstage communal improviser— for, unlike the others, one now knew the script, one knew the inevitable future. While still here on the unredeemed earth, a Marxist (even, perhaps especially, an American Marxist of a small pridefully pure variety, with no mass movement behind him or her) is also already part of the elect, protected from the defeats—even the death—one suffered now, because, by dialectics, one could, in one's mind, savor the paradise of the future, and look back on the present as if one had survived it.

One was promised that by one's adherence to this doctrine one was cleansed—and there was a tincture of this desire for redemption added to radicalism (of the left and right) in the Sixties, as it had been at other times in America's history as well (washed in the blood of . . . ? one's own, of course, but others' more copiously). Political action was a religious action that would cleanse one of guilt, for even if one was not part of the owning class, one had sinned by being a member of the comfortable American middle class. This is a perhaps almost inevitable confusion of the realms of politics and religion, for once such basic matters as the remaking of oneself and humanity are contemplated, one becomes the not-quite-human ally—or demiurge—of the god History. But this confusion of realms can be a terrible one, for one then might not notice the pain unto death that one caused others in the process of seeking atonement with one's god. There are political ends that political sacrifice is not worth, but under the crushing implacable interdiction of one's conscience there seems no sacrifice that one shouldn't make for atonement.

And soon, perhaps sacrifices were sought out, so that one might continue to feel oneself aligned with "the forces of history." History's end was known; it was community and freedom reconciled; and to achieve this end History demanded sacrifice. (Because it demanded sacrifices it *must* be a god!) But History is an unstable master, and Marxist theory is not truly *outside* the process that it supposedly controls. So one's willingness to make sacrifice was perhaps necessary to hallow the cause, make it appear sacred and certain, as well as to show that one was certainly part of the elect. That describes a small portion of the American Left—or of the American Right, for that matter—but a part easily available to frighten others. And the effects of their excesses enter our post-modern irony, our fear of conflict, becoming a way to discredit anyone who uses the word "justice," to justify his or her action.

There was on the part of most of the left an examination of whether Marx's paradigm applied (no matter how transformed); a sense of the tyranny that had been wrought in his name (and why); there was, even in the Sixties, a suspicion that there were (within or outside Marxism) no stable, eternal values, and the knowledge that the morality that wasn't quite firmly *there* in Marx's text is given the illusion of being present by the sacrifices one offered—of oneself, and of others—as if the blood one offered proved the truth of what was offered blood. In forming an understanding of Marx's errors, Marx was read, so to speak, by Freud and by Nietzsche.

Nietzsche gave the most forceful (as well as the most genuinely, if savagely, playful) rendering in modern times of the effects of the absence of God as a moral guide, and the causes of this absence, and the consequence: that the more courageous we are in acknowledging the absence of God, the more we might also be frighteningly unruly in our projects, free to take whatever shape whim suggests. History, perhaps, would *not* decide; or guide; and it could justify nothing. Nietzsche's directive is that we should make our whims difficult, rare, beautiful; and "beautiful" should mean that which excites oneself and others to further difficult creation—world, and whim, without end.

Both Marx and Freud were, by contrast to Nietzsche, often believers not in whim, but in science. As scientists—when they saw themselves as scientists—what they had discovered was, they thought, empirical truth, and the efforts they urged us to were no more (or less!) than the recognition of human nature's necessities.

Still, Marx and Freud teach a divided lesson about this "nature." On the one hand, Marx says, humanity makes itself. Our needs, our desires, our sense of our rights and possibilities, have changed many times over the course of our collective and our personal history, and they can change again. In this vision, our always contradictory nature poses us questions that we have answered in ever-new ways in the permanent revolution that is human life. By contrast, in the "scientific" (the "positivist") Marx and Freud, there is a belief that human nature is not an interrogation but a guide, and our task is simply to discover and make ourselves congruent with our inevitable necessities. Marx's "anthropology"—his conviction that people have always quested for an even-sided development of their productive powers—is thin in content, but crucial to his thought, for that anthropology is, finally, the "ought" of his work, why one *must* act to bring about the new society. *That* society will allow for the *proper* development of human nature, what Marx calls our "species essence." This "even-sided development" of an individual's many gifts requires, as stage and material, a bountiful social world. But a *different* social world from any we have known. All previous societies, because of scarcity and oppression, skewed us from our happy possibilities, set us against one another, and distorted us. If we are "distorted," then we must have a natural form. (But what if our natures are more fundamentally divided, what if we sometimes freely *choose* pain, choose the destruction of our worldly goods? That way lies the riddle posed by de Sade's and Dostoyevsky's and Nietzsche's ideas. Can we imagine a social world that could allow—and even fully *use,* in our work and our acts of generosity—our defiant sado-masochistic drives, our perverse, hyperbolic assertions of freedom?)

Freud, the revolutionary, or at least the reformist Freud, thought that an outmoded and deceitful morality kept us from seeing what we actually did, made us turn the present into a version of the past, a new edition, Freud called it, of old conflicts—kept us from grasping the new possibilities that confronted us. In *this* Freud, human nature was a series of questions or themes that human life might embody in new ways with a new morality. Freud's work shows "perverse" sexuality using the same themes and symbols as "normal," genitally organized, sexuality, so "normal" isn't so much a healthy matching of organs with meanings as a conventional one. (Happiness now, Freud argues, usually lies along the conventional path. But that is a far from inevitable matter. We could, for example, have different symbols for futurity than children, a different structure for child-raising than conventional families.) If we have a "human nature" here, it is in our penchant to elaborate and to live endlessly fantastical, but not equally satisfying, versions of our answers, and perhaps the most satisfying "answers" are not the more sensible or more moderate ones, but those that allow us to embody our instinctual contradictions more profoundly, more fully.

But when we try to imagine new conventions, a new morality, Freud, the conservative, confronts us with seductive Possibility's inevitable conclusion and limit in iron Necessity. Here our nature not only provides themes, it insists on plot and character. *This* Freud's apprehension of human nature leads him to say that "anatomy is fate," and write as if he knew what that fate is, not merely identifying masculinity with activity and femininity with passivity, but writing as if he knows *what* those qualities must always mean, how they *must* manifest themselves. (*Must* manifest themselves, that is, if we are to have even a modicum of contentment.) The magisterial, conservative Freud is possessor of the knowledge of human nature; he describes health as self-chosen renunciation of impossible desires and implacable grievances, so that one might, however regretfully, take one's already ordained (ordained by our nature, our anatomy) place in the life cycle, a story whose plot cannot change very much.

So Marx and Freud vacillate between a nature that poses questions to life, and a nature that is stern teacher. One might almost say that it was the institutions that claim to embody Freud and Marx's work that imposed a single-minded idea of the answers, the plot our lives must embody, on their founders' more equivocal vision of the questions our nature asks. To maintain their power over us, the guardians of the institutions require a single authoritative view of our nature to which our life, with their *help,* must be made to conform.

But Nietzsche threw the quadrant "nature" overboard, and imagined our modernity more grandly, and with another spirit, perhaps amoral, perhaps perverse—but now by what standard of human nature can one call it that? Our essence, Nietzsche said, is unknown because it doesn't exist. God and Nature are dead, and human nature is just a jejune stand-in for the guidance of the Law once given by the now absconded God.

Good—one might say, a trifle glibly—then our "nature" is nature no longer; it is of our making, and we are free to illuminate or transform it with hallucinogens, to seek out blissful anodynes or extremities of suffering. The self was made and can be endlessly remade. In the Sixties, both the American Left and the "counterculture"—realms not always divisible—included many attempts at self-transformation, of consciousness-raising and mind-blowing, that, as if Nietzsche were their half-hidden forebear, sought no guidance as to their goals beyond what might "feel right" to the experimenter. But, as one might expect from America, even the apparent hedonism of the "counterculture" had found its original impetus in morality. "Feels right" had meant that one enacted now the attitude towards one's comrades and towards the self that was to become universal if the action succeeded.

Black and white civil rights workers as they got off the bus to be greeted by Southern sheriffs, and Southern blacks by the simple but enormous act of registering to vote, had shown that one might discover one's power and one's beloved community in the very process of building it. The movement that took its impetus and its direction from those events tried to find areas of implacable opposition (even, sometimes, where none existed), in order to ensure the feeling of wholeness and courage, of being on the right track, that can come from such opposition. The elaborating, and living, of such decided actions—community now, empowerment now, paradise now—was meant to ensure that the future and its goals were of one's own making, not granted or guided by an external power, whether called the party, or the therapist, or the state.

The belief that only what one feels on the pulses is true—for in the absence of God could there be other guarantees of truth?—expresses, in part, a hidden yearning to force the coming of the Messiah, and, in part, the impatience of those who couldn't tolerate any more delayed gratification. But most of all it's the recognition (more Nietzschean than Marxist) that there may be no transcendental certainties, in theory or in morality, no other assurance beyond one's feeling that one will successfully reach one's goal, or that the goal is worth reaching. But then, a more thoroughgoing reader of Nietzsche might ask, why should one's feeling be more reliable than God's revelation? Or perhaps Nietzsche, too, turns his spade here: One simply has either a noble will, and its beautiful action-provoking sentiments, or one has the slave's will, with its fear, resentment, and twisted machinations.

The demand, for palpable self-transformation, for inner feeling as the test of authenticity in one's life, incited the ecstasy of the sexually liberated, even the perverse, the formation of the nonhierarchical community, the experimentation with the expanded or raised or blown consciousness. In such efforts, you don't know how much of the future you can engorge now, how far you can go, until you go too far—an attitude that is ill-suited to political action, if that is thought of not as tragic foolishness but as the taking of state power, of the instituting of new social arrangements.

"Authenticity" as the embodying now, being guided now, by all of one's vital individual differences from a deadening larger society had its place (along with a desire to have one's piece of America's cherry pie) in such ideas as "black power." But this special valuing of one's distinctive feelings, and one's feeling of distinctiveness—even if one recognized, as ethnic and racial advocates often forget, that it, too, was made, was a social product and so far from ineradicable—became, soon enough, the countercultural idea that whatever feels good to you is right. Its original moral impulse—to live the transformed life—was often lost, along with any sense that a moral and social dimension were needed. The self and its appetites, whose re-creation was once one's task, became instead, as it already existed, the whole world.

These experiments led to a repugnance on the part of the vast majority of one's countrymen, and, for the participants themselves, often led to a terror at the possibilities revealed—

if not a positive unhingement. Once you discover you've gone too far, there is, say the empty Little Orphan Annie eyes on Berkeley's Telegraph Avenue, no going back. But fear of disorder isn't sufficient to make God reestablish an ordered world of ineradicable meanings—though it may lead to a querulous conservatism, an insistence that one *must* have such a world.

Knowing our whimsical instability, yet fearing it, has not only led to conservative polemics, it has also germinated a weak version of Nietzsche that has become a comfortable part of our post-modernism, a half-acceptance of our freedom. Nietzsche's terrifying discovery that there may be no genuine "self," only masks to wear, becomes our contemporary costume show. We can take any form, but we usually take the forms of the past—thus post-modern retro-style. History, no longer the commanding Marxist God of implacable necessities, has become instead a panoply of lifestyles to purchase, an inventory of deceptions for our ironic use. Nietzsche's admonition that the self is a mask that one must carve becomes the glad lies (for what is truth?) of marketing, of well-packaged commodities. Politics, leisure, even morality are all to be seen "aesthetically," masochistically enjoyed as varieties of deception, forms of entertainment. Nietzsche now seems not the dangerous anti-Christ he thought himself, but the philosopher of the consumer society and the oral stage of development, the baby's way of expressing preference as the beginning and end of thought: "I like this, I don't like that. I spit that out."

This "version" of Nietzsche's thought has something to do with the protected conditions of our lives, with a state well and brilliantly organized for a freedom of choice in consumption ("I spit this out. I *buy* this."). Perhaps this liberalism leads, as most European commentators since Tocqueville have said, to a thinness, a lack of layering or deep commitments in

American personality; we change the channel or the town; and, in any case, the town isn't there anymore. Indeed we may have come to lack values and rights we would die for, as we lack, one hopes, purchases we would die for. (Except our right—no small one—to manufacture and to purchase.) And even our interest in the grand projects of self and social transformation may come to seem to us like another kind of purchase, ornaments to a "lifestyle." But what do our purchases ornament? Nothing? A socially created self without essence? All in all, one may prefer *not* to see oneself as wearing a mask that has *nothing* beneath it but the unguided will itself. One might prefer a version of the self as at least a tasteful stylist and consumer, and the mask as a well-chosen ornament.

The profundity of the aesthetic sense, Nietzsche thought, would be sufficient to lead the lonely creator back, finally, to art's greatest challenge, self-transformation—the will cutting into the self, carving the mask, each stroke a reshaping, and so the demise as well, of one's previous personality. Instead, today one imagines one has a nubbin of a static, essential self, constantly reornamented with current fashions. Fashion is tragic self-transformation become the manifold opportunities of taste. We wish to grasp the possibilities of the present, to be (in Rimbaud's phrase) absolutely modern, but we have settled for grasping the possibility of purchasing the present, a present not communally or individually made by us, but consumed by each one, worn by each one alone (yet with an implied group of fashionable cohorts, in the pages of the magazine, or at some numinous imagined restaurant). The designer's name on the patch indicates that we know life is replete with opportunities for self-expression, for stylization. But, anxious and to some degree impotent, worn out or narrowed by the work that we specialize in, we require others to perform that stylization for us and reassure us of its excellence. Instead of self-making, we fashionable ones can offer ourselves self-congratulations. We are in the "vanguard," but it isn't anymore our own feeling or the party and its slogans that guarantees that status, but the designer's name, and his advertisements, which, like the party propaganda endlessly reiterated, says "I am in advance of the position that others will occupy, part of the elect, not saved perhaps, but not, God forbid, in bad taste." (Both the Party and couturiers have new lines.)

The desire to be fashionable is at the heart of the post-modern ethos—where to be substantial is to be seen. When one is not seen (and at the best places), one doesn't exist. In an image-saturated society only those appearances that are made to appear on a screen count as real. (However, one must add that in a Christian society only those appearances that *don't* appear count as real, only the charity done where no one can see counts as real charity. Thus the uneasiness of our desire.) Most of us won't be famous, won't be seen and so be real, even for fifteen minutes. Fame may be our society's most prized scarce good—necessarily scarce, because if *you* are being watched, *I'm* not. But, at least, we can each buy something from the bazaar, we can wear what those on T.V. wear. Alas, poor shirt, at once so glamorous and so tawdry, once we buy it, it is no longer on screen, and so no longer real, able to cover me—the emperor's story reversed—with visibility.

There is a tantalizingly diabolical embodiment of this in cable T.V.'s "Home Shopping Club." The spectacles' wares are shown on T.V. by a pitchman, and a few lucky buyers, the more regular customers, are heard—but not shown, of course—as they phone in their orders. For a few magic moments, they chat with the salesmen about the joy given them by their recently acquired purchases. So as they buy, they are *almost* on the air, as if they were sitting next to Oprah, just off screen, only their voices present, as if, maybe with their next purchase, they might move down the couch and their bodies, too, might appear. . . .

This uncertainty about one's reality is, Freud would say, hysteria. It is, finally, an uncertainty about gender, the linch pin, he thought, on which the stable personality is organized. The psychoanalyst Serge Leclaire has memorably phrased the hysteric's problem as his constant questioning of himself and the world, as if he were with every action asking, "Am I a man or a woman?" Fashion, with its extremity of stylization, offers a hyperbolic masculinity or femininity, whose overstatement also reveals a denial of one's gender. (For we are, Freud argues, each inherently bisexual. So whichever gender we choose to represent, we do so ambivalently.) Fashion provides a drug for one's anxiety ("Just look! I am so much this sex!" Or, "Please admire this irony, I am really *not* this sex!"). Yet the costume makes one more anxious, for one only ambivalently wants whatever it asserts. And fashion keeps all trapped within the orbit of its questions and its answers, not going deeper into what *produces* gender. But, why should we, if that deeper asking can only lead to a more painful, more poignant anxiety, a more resounding emptiness?

If one could bear that deeper anxiety, that recognition that one has no essence, that the personality is constructed, then the interrogation of values, of gender, of reality itself as merely a "convention" could, Nietzsche thought, become the ground not only of irony but of new creation. This would be, he thought, hard, difficult, violent work. Violence, Nietzsche, like Freud, saw was inevitable. Our own age is violent and cruel, but denies what its hands do (and secretly, resentfully, enjoys); it calls cruelty morality. Nietzsche valued most those societies—the Greeks of the tragic age, the Hebrews—which were rich and open in their cruelty, for that meant, too, he thought, that violence might be used for new and admirable creation.

But what shape should those creations take? This alternative Nietzsche quite properly terrifies. If there is no god to guide one's creations but one's taste, then what if one has a taste for blood? What if the greatest ecstasy I can imagine is the ecstasy of murder? By 1974, as "the Sixties" ended, each night's news could make one feel surrounded by murderers—the state, with its many instruments of violence (armies and agents, TAC squads and SWAT teams), the wild boys and girls of the left, and the drug-driven squeaky loons of the desert fringe. (And now, has our capacity for murder disappeared—or even abated?) One was drawn to a Nietzschean style (whether one knew his name or not) by its incitement to search out actions that were not to be justified by the audience, or even by the future they brought about, but by the ecstasy of self-transformation that they created now. But what of those who disdain the difficulties of self-making, and experience only the quasi-ecstasy of drugs or the thrill of the drive-by shooting? How can we tell a true god, a true ecstasy, from a false one?

Nietzsche replies that the noble wants conflict among equals; he collects his debts; enjoys the punishment he inflicts; *has done*. The resentful wants an audience, wants to make the other's pain endless, invents not combat but torture; for the cries of the tormented are the only recognition of his excellence, or even his existence, that the resentful will ever receive. (The "Final Solution" would surely have found new victims.) Like the hysteric that Freud describes (or the slave of fashion), the slavish will thirsts for recognition, for the audience's acknowledgement of its substantiality. The noble, by contrast, has an ego so strong that he can lose it; and for him only a total loss will do, one where the old self is necessarily destroyed by the symbolic hammer blows that are part of the sculpting of a new self. So Nietzsche reinterprets tragedy as the inevitably mingled experience of self-loss and self-creation, where the old Adam goes under as a new self is created. In this time of peace and plenty, Nietzsche incites us to transform our work into an activity in which we might fully spend ourselves, go under and be reborn, again and again changing ourselves into something strange and beautiful. (Nietzsche's vision may be too grand and abstract to offer much guidance. It's hard to match his aphorisms to part-time work at McDonald's, without his words becoming simply an aristocratic curse. Yet I don't think we have improved upon his severe incitements or his questions.)

Nietzsche thought that only a full, a tragic loss would satisfy, and would momentarily make manifest his "god"—the procreative lust of the world, the Will to Power—which is worth one's own continued activity, which, in the moment of tragic going-under, both guides one's hand, and is one's hand. In such moments of ecstatic, tragic loss of self there is no one present to care for an audience's applause.

Aesthetics without an audience? The absence of audience may distinguish between the noble and the slave, but what will prevent the slave from disastrously burlesquing the noble will? The drug addict parodies reshaping the self by obliterating it, and those not strong enough to be tragic actors can always be lured to mimic the noble through orgies of destruction of others—rather than the tragedy of self re-creation. What is society to do with such kill-crazy people who are incapable of living up to Nietzsche's aesthetic standards? Nietzsche's distinction between the self-transforming noble and the buffoonish killer, his aesthetic injunction to use one's violence to live a tragic life of self-transformation, may be an insufficient substitute for the moral imperative to restrain one's violence. But our moral imperatives, too, have repeatedly shown their weakness this century, even as our technological ability to magnify that violence has increased. If morality has failed us, then we still must resolve the question of what is to be done with our inevitably violent will. (Or do we imagine that our capacity for murder has disappeared?) Nietzsche was not the apostle of violence, although he thought violence was the inevitable blood red thread that, in action and in suffering, forms life. Violence, Nietzsche thought, must be *shaped.* But how can we use our violence in our work, or lead it to its true object in self-transformation, if we don't acknowledge its presence? The critic Robert Warshow, in writing about Westerns, noted how aware America's popular artists seem to be of the inevitability of violence, while well-meaning critics train themselves "to be shocked or bored by cultural images of violence. . . . This . . . is a virtue, but like many virtues it involves . . . willful blindness and it encourages hypocrisy." The plots and figures—like the "private eye" and the "gunfighter"—that popular artists have elaborated are too literal minded in their idea of violence (never work, always guns), too simple both in their inner life and in the clear evil they face, but they are at least meant to give some style and warrant to the expression of a violence that life cannot avoid. Western movies are rarely made anymore, I think, not because we lack love for our country's myths, but because the gunfighter is no longer a figure who can embody justified violence, nor can he contain or stylize our deathly energies; when high noon came, he couldn't face down the atomic bomb. In our popular art, mythic history has been replaced by a fantasy that seems at once sweeter, more jokey, and less convincing—laser-swords in space and a time long ago and far away. And justified violence has been superseded by Rambo, a resentful fantasy of revenge and mayhem.

Nietzsche, like Freud, thought that the weight of our unacknowledged sadistic desires would show itself in a deadening of our taste for life, and then explode in a misplaced love of the knife; the gun; the instruments of torture; the camps; the ovens . . . Can Nietzsche's understanding be purged of, protected from, the ecstasy of destruction? A misinterpretation, Nietzsche says, of what the body truly wants. What we truly want is work as a mental war; the self struggling to be self-transformed; the body self-transformed; what we settle for is the body cutting into other bodies.

Nietzsche offers only the dark cup; instead of security—either the imaginary security of being part of the Marxist elect, the religiously saved, the band of the fully psychoanalyzed, or the more substantial security of the good career—he offers the tragic sense of life. We accumulate for security or consume for comfort when we do not have the courage to consume *ourselves* in the self-forgetfulness of ecstatic, self-making activity. But Nietzsche's high vaunting of the noble will that would seek no justification outside itself, that craved action to the point of self-destruction, and his aesthetization of politics (for politics was to be guided not by morality, but by the noble beauty it created), these became bones for the skeleton of fascism. The tragic sense seems too slender a thread to guide us through the maze of our collective or individual histories. Yet what other source is there by which a guiding truth might be compelled to speak?

Nietzsche's fundamental questions are still our questions to answer—where do the gods (the values, the code) come from that can shape our sadism and gratify our thirst for satisfying action? What action, if not ecstatic tragic action—the work in which one is utterly spent and remade—will provide that communion with the ongoing (ah, but meaningless?) procreative lust of the world? (It is an immersion we long for. Denied it in work, we will seek its parody in fast cars, loud movies, icy drugs.) And what will give that endless movement meaning (for we must, as he reminds us, have meaning)? Can we create for ourselves—only half-forgetting our own role in the creation—a new god to guide us? How, in a world without transcendent truth, can one tell a challenging noble god from a false one? These riddles our "weak" post-modern Nietzscheanism has turned away from without answering.

Perhaps, Freud thought, the answers might come from a more thoroughgoing examination of our personal histories. The artistic question of what *I* find beautiful, or the question that fashion lies about (am *I* a man or a woman?), or the question of tragedy (what gives one a self?), followed through the labyrinth of one's own past, leads, Freud thought, to the presiding gods whose struggle forms our life's themes, the gods of eros and death. The instincts are the gods whose struggle *is* our deepest "self," whose words interrupt our chatter and make our speech into symptoms, into that invaluable broken stutter, which is, if only we had ears to hear, the voice of those whose shapes also haunt our dreams. (That is to say that analysis might allow us to enter, from moment to moment, that place where the contradictions of one's life are felt as what inevitably constitutes one, that realm once called tragic.)

Through Freud's work one might learn to delineate in one's

choice of partners, in the slips of the tongue and in the vows taken, the god, Eros, who presides over our moments of bodily satisfaction, of union. Through this searching examination of our own history, we might finally learn to name our task, the questions to which our lives will endlessly respond. Pleasure is sexual pleasure, and it is of the body. This did not mean, precisely, the body as opposed to the mind, *for the mind, too, is of the body*—the mind's work is making symbolic expressions of the instincts' desire. Sublimation is not simply repression; and culture could, Freud thought, in the hopeful decades before the First World War, be made somewhat more satisfying without ceasing to be culture. (Has this opportunity come again?)

This led, for some of Freud's followers and for many in the Sixties' counterculture—call them the Party of Pleasure—to grander hopes than Freud would have allowed. The dream, for example, that, guided by psychoanalysis, a new consciousness might be created, one that did not dryly, on the couch or in the library, unriddle the sexual dimension of culture, but would experience that connection at each moment. Seen through Freud's spectacles, culture is symbols—a cigar is *never* just a cigar—which allow us to enact our union with others and with nature; yet we do not *feel* that union, that utopian, polymorphous internationale that would include the whole of creation. If one felt at that "bodily" level one's joining to the symbols one used, felt both hatred and love, then each symbol, as it was linked with one's body (loved, eaten, incorporated), might transform one. But to have such activity would itself require a rebirth, a self not afraid of the constant going-under of the symbolic life. One would experience death (and use one's death instinct) not as the end of life, or as the inner-directed force of a morality that keeps one rigid, but in one's constant transformation.

All this has, indeed, an improbable, countercultural (now "new age") sound. For a change in the psyche is also the cause of pain. Death, even as change, is feared by the ego, and our flight from death, as much as our longings for union, has helped shape the symbols our egos have fixed themselves upon, those outer monuments that are meant to make us immortal, that inner rigidity that uses the energy of the death instinct for a morality that restrains the self, saving it back from change. The self-transformation we longed for, and sometimes glancingly experienced in the Sixties, will always also be felt as the *death* of the old self, and so will always create an almost overwhelming anxiety. The sense that the body politic and one's own body are fragmenting leads to new repression (to hold the self together), new distortion of the possibilities and agents of change. But what if one *doesn't* feel that connection to nature and to culture? Will the world come to seem, as our slang repeatedly reminds us, so much shit—a screen on which to project all in oneself to which one doesn't wish to acknowledge connection, all one wishes to conquer, to destroy?

So in imagining some new vision of connectedness, one must not ignore Eros's implacable antagonist, Death. We fear change (even our ecstasies), for we fear death, and misapprehend change as the end of life. Still, that deathly force in us, which wishes to destroy and to die, must indeed be restrained—or one should say, following Nietzsche, violence must be *shaped* (and violence, too, is the means by which it is shaped). To avoid a violence that might crush the social world, or a death-drive that might destroy the self, one now uses death by turning it against one's own body, not as suicide but as morality.

So arises civilization's inevitable uneasiness, for this compromise—which uses death as morality to build barriers against eros—satisfies neither god. (And the more we restrain our outward-directed violence, the more deathly energy conscience has to use against the self, as morality and guilt.) The death instinct, Freud imagined, is violence—directed at the self, as guilt, or at the world—and we fear it. But we also, inevitably, long for it; simply repressed, Nietzsche and Freud agree, it will return in orgies of destruction. And the deepest erotic claims of the human body, not for spectacle, but for care and for connection—claims dangerously ignored, I think, this last decade—if frustrated and unsatisfied, will, Caliban-like, be diverted by the energy of the death instinct to join in a curse on life. Freud's great work, *Civilization and Its Discontents,* ends in a wan (and so far unanswered) prayer to Eros, that perhaps—or so I imagine it—the sources of pleasure might be increased, that the energy of death might be bound up with pleasure, that we might create work for ourselves that uses death by allowing a fuller loss, a more complete expenditure of the self, and find our satisfaction not in destroying the world, but in reshaping the world and the self: "Men have gained control over the forces of nature to such an extent that with their help they would have no difficulty in exterminating one another to the last man. They know this, and hence comes a large part of their current unrest, their unhappiness and their mood of anxiety. And now it is to be expected that the other of the two 'Heavenly Powers,' eternal Eros, will make an effort to assert himself in the struggle with his equally immortal adversary. But who can foresee with what success and with what result."

Freud's work can give Marx's and Nietzsche's ideas a bodily fulfillment, one that could help answer Freud's own prayer to eros. The communion that Marx imagines must be felt as a *bodily* connection to others: for we wish both to give and to receive care, to be nourished, and to provide nourishment. Nietzsche's "will to power" is the strong braiding of the drives of love and death. So the endless self-satisfying activity that Nietzsche imagines would be work that—in culture, through symbols—expresses the instincts, that satisfies and transforms the body by connecting it with other bodies. But for this fulfillment we require still a new dispensation, a new authority—and will it be a new structure? a god? a new sense of solidarity?—that will help shape our violence, give meaning to our self-sacrifice, that will hold us even as we are being, from moment to moment, reborn, and so make our anxiety bearable. The paradox, then, is that both pleasure and transformation come from symbolic joinings, but to be courageous enough to engage in ecstatic transformative acts, we must feel *already* joined to the world, already held by it. Without that, our anxiety will make us prey to all the false gods who promise not activity but immortality, and incite the bloody orgy, piling the corpses before them.

Freud may have instruction still to give about the body's true needs, and he may have insights still to offer to a renewed political imagination. But, as with Nietzsche, we have constructed instead our own post-modern Freud to turn from the task of finding satisfaction (or to pretend that history is over, its tasks already accomplished, its deepest satisfactions attained). Instead of curing life of its illness (its fear of ecstasy which is its fear of death), psychoanalysis declares life itself the illness, one that requires continual analysis. Trained by Freud, one sees that the obsessive strength of one's attractions comes from one's unassimilated, unacknowledged past. Before analysis, one foolishly thinks one is refinding a lost love. The patient studies this as it happens in the transference, when he confuses the analyst with the parent and, by mistake, loves him or her. He then learns to find such mistakes in all his passions. After analysis (but is there an after analysis?) one should feel one's attractions only distantly—as if watching television. All things being equal, then, why choose anything in particular or hold to anything for long? Why not change the station? Fear—and one wouldn't want to gainsay a sensible fear!—and weak attachments to the point of indifference are attitudes that form the ethos of our current condition. And though Freud's work may help us to account for our fear, it has not yet helped us to overcome it—except in the analysis interminable.

But I think we can uncover, through the theories of Freud and the other patriarchs, a deeper idea of the conflicts that made our past—rather than settling for a fetishistic or ironic quoting of the past, as do neo-conservative philosophers and some post-modern architects. If there are archetypes, or recurrent themes or motifs, a human nature to instruct one, it will be found, I think, not in Jungian images, or the vernacular decorations of Las Vegas buildings, but in the Freudian *questions,* the interrogations—like the hysteric's am I a man or a woman?—that the curve of one's life embodies. The way forward, I think, is to see how the patriarchs' projects of self-understanding can themselves be taken up again *as questions* as the best contemporary thought does, so we might recapture our history not as burden but as making, and so remake ourselves. This must, of course, happen at the most basic levels, those where we hardly suspect that a "making" has occurred, where nature, so to speak, seems most natural. Feminism, for example, that vital extension of modern thought—the end of the illusion that patriarchy was our exclusive genesis—shows us that we must first grasp ourselves not as "he" or "she." The infant is not yet gendered as *we* understand that. The baby biped is only a bundle of wants—an "it," says Freud, an active or passive will, says Nietzsche, a place in the process of production, says Marx—with a certain set of organs. There will always be a biological difference between male and female. But what that difference *means* is culturally made and could be made very differently. And it is in part the greatness of these authors' works that they can often be read, using their own terms, *against* their patriarchal prejudices to help us reimagine that making. These thinkers can be turned back on themselves to elucidate their own failures. Freud, too, can be psychoanalyzed.

A new post-modern (or continuation of the modern) that had the bracing tang of their work, a post-modern that was not simply chastened or ironic, might, I think, come out of that enterprise. We can, a little while longer, try to continue to believe in the providence of the market (and betray by our gestures that we do not believe); try to mis-remember the modern project, as if we had already answered the patriarchs' questions—turning Nietzsche into a purveyor of a happy masochistic aesthetic where we are connoisseurs of falsity, or making Freud the doctor who turned life into a sickness. Or we can with sober senses once again enter into the spirit of their work and extend it, guided still by our American desire for a union that is of this earth, one that is never complete "fusion" but always momentary, always restless, dissatisfied, always possibly "more perfect," a union that is always only almost one. In that way we might gain some instruction on how to continue the interrupted project to embody and re-shape our violence and our love, our new possibilities for destruction and for connection, for fulfilling work and for profounder, more vivid lives.

ON GIVING
BIRTH TO ONE'S
OWN MOTHER

☐   When I think about the story of my writing life, I like to use clinical names with their somber consulting room air and almost scientific prestige. *Hysteric, depressive, obsessive, schizoid.* I try the names on my character, the way one puts on astrological signs, or medieval humors, or those brief descriptions of Chinese mythologies—born in the year of the Rat, you should marry a Dragon—on the tea-stained place mat of the local Szechuan restaurant. In the clinical names or the place mat's mythology, I'm looking for a clue to my *fate*—not who my wife should be, but what my next story should be, so that its theme might be mine, *inevitably,* to write. I think of these clinical types as if they were characters put under a curse by the uninvited guest at the christening, or the troll who stole one's child in return for the secret to weaving flax into gold. And, as in a fairy tale, the curse can be turned into a task— find the way through the forest, the name of the troll, the memory of the texture of your mother's cloth coat. The task of answering that question is one's fate—the story that is profound because you *have* to tell it—and so the curse becomes a question; a fate, is, for a writer (or so I hope) a blessing.

Each clinical type, of course, has its own question to pursue, as it moves towards . . . wholeness? health? Even to say "health" sounds too grand. Perhaps health is just to live one's own question fully, to find new facets to one's question at each stage of life—and not, simply, boringly, to repeat oneself.

Let me show you what I mean by telling you the fairy tale of the hysteric, the character with which Freud began the creation of psychoanalysis. Theatrical in the way he or she presents herself, the hysteric demands attention. (He *or* she—for Freud discovered that hysteria wasn't just a privilege of women, a matter of organs, of a wandering womb, but a matter of fantasies about organs, imaginings that either men or women might have.) Perhaps the future hysteric's parents, that crucial out-of-town tryout for adulthood, weren't a very attentive audience. So the hysterics made their gestures broader. Now the body is pushed up; pumped out; low cut; heavily advertised. They mean to attract, but if you are attracted, you find that the same drama simply repeats itself: their encouragement, your request, their refusal (but please, do, ask again). If you do make love, you feel your lover isn't lost in the act, but performing. As in some theaters, you may feel the actor, the hysteric, doesn't, really, mean what he says. But that's wrong. He means to attract, but what he truly wants is not your company in bed, but your regard. For when he's not being looked at, he's unsure who he is, and he falls into a dark abyss of anxiety, of loss of self.

The French psychoanalyst Serge Leclair framed the hysteric's question—his theme—as, "Am I a man or a woman?" The hysteric shills viewers into the theater, for they reassure, by their attraction, that s/he is a plausible man or woman. But if, deeply attracted, you want to come backstage, then the hysteric's anxiety is increased. Intimacy might lead to his being called an impostor. (Who am I? *What* am I?) So an affair with a hysteric is rarely consummated.

There are elements of the hysteric's attitude in any artist's character, but the good artist has a small, cold margin of freedom that allows him to study his actions. Reading the book of himself, he gains insight into the ways characters might dramatize themselves; he learns something, too, about keeping an audience's attention. (Ah, if a reader looks away, that is *truly* awful!) But when a writer is *trapped* within his hysteria, then he deals in shocks only, and his habitual mode is a shallow melodrama. We rush on from page to page, investing our attention, our emotion, only to toss the book aside at the end, unsatisfied. Not because we want a good book to tidy everything up; rather, we want the questions the plot proposed, the ones that drove us on, to open into more questions, in an ever-widening context that interrogates us and our lives. A bad hysterical book brutally *insists* on its conclusions: This is the dead body; this is the murderer; the end. The good book becomes, in Wildean play, ever more involving, for the writer trusts the body of his material to sustain our interest. An ending, a consummation, isn't a conclusion, and the affair between writer and reader becomes a marriage.

The hysteric's question, "Am I a man or a woman?" is surely a great theme for an artist. Who can ever know the final answer to such a profound question? And this is an especially exciting era for a hysteric, for so many of us now share his quizzical uncertainty about gender. In works like those of the photographer Cindy Sherman, who disguises and photographs herself in slightly off-kilter "fashion layouts," in "movie stills," in "fairy tales," we begin to see the ways that being a man or a woman is a socially made construct—not a matter of organs but of what those organs are made, collectively and individually, to mean. (Is a phallus a sword, a bridge, a way back to the womb? And what does a womb mean? And why?) The hysteric's question can illuminate the life we make together—if, that is, the artist can turn the question this way and that, be, playfully, sometimes man, sometimes woman (as his stories demand), and nothing forever. He can use the question, if he does not *have* to have the story come out a certain way, if he doesn't feel that his life depends on your taking him for his idea of a man.

But the character type that interests me most is the depressive. (Beware—as Eliot wrote, when a poet writes criticism his real goal is to justify his own sensibility.) We melancholiacs are the tribe that suffers the curse of *perpetual* mourning. We slouch slowly outside the festivals of life. For a moment, we finish grieving, our mood lightens, we caper antically. Yet we forever find occasions to mourn anew. Someone has *always* just left us, or is about to leave, and faced with that loss—even an argument with someone we love, a flick of the eyes over our shoulder as we speak together at a party, a promised phone call not received—we are utterly cast down. The world, then, is well described by Kafka, as "a suicidal thought in the mind of God," and helpless, unprotected, we fall through infinite, empty space.

And your turning away (we'll be the first to admit) is our fault, and we feel awful about what wretches we are. We have a penchant in our life, and our work, for judgment (moral, psychological). Our self-judgment even has a warm, almost erotic quality, like the guilt of the characters in Bernard Malamud's sour-rye stories.

Psychiatrists—I draw here on Anthony Storr's excellent, humane handbook for beginning clinicians, *The Art of Psychotherapy*—conjecture that the depressive may have had a long time of helpless dependence as an infant, perhaps because of sickness. Perhaps, too, his parents were not always—always, always, *always!*—adoring. Sometimes they looked away. *Why have they looked away? What displeased them? And how can I possibly care for myself without them?* To keep these gods' regard and protection, the child strives to be perfect.

And such parents *must* be gods. Or how can the child be sure they can protect him? The sickly child fears that he suffers by comparison with others; without his parents' approval to buoy him up he finds it impossible to think well of himself. Only a god's choosing him could make him feel sufficiently special to overcome his sense of inadequacy. I am reminded, here, of my other tribe, the Chosen People—chosen by God to obey his difficult Law, making us alternately sublime and utterly worthless. Such hyperbole provides a temporary stay against depression, one that becomes part of any tribe member's (and any writer's) tools: a way to insist that one has been chosen to write, and that one's characters are worth the reader's attention. But if one fails, writes badly, one is worthless, abandoned by God and the reader, in an infinite, empty desert.

To keep his parents' good opinion, the depressive child learns to fulfill *their* half-hidden emotional needs. A useful lesson for a future writer: *to imagine what others feel,* the nub of creating his characters. But, in his life, he may find himself imprisoned within this talent, so afraid of loss that he not only feels with others, but is crushed by *their* feelings, by his need to restore what his loved ones have been denied. D. H. Lawrence's story "The Rocking Horse Winner" is a chilling metaphor for this: The little boy, rocking desperately on his toy horse, manages to conjure the names of future winners for his unhappy parents.

Sometimes, the depressive feels so swamped by others' requirements that he flees, perhaps to his room, perhaps to write. There, in his imagined world, he is free. Characters he creates need not be placated; a whole town can be washed away by a flood if one wishes. In his dragon world, no longer helpless, he may accomplish satisfying prodigies of creation and destruction. Writing—just push the pages under the door—becomes an almost safe way to connect with others, and, perhaps, win their oh so necessary golden opinion.

But only perhaps. To finish, to publish, leaves one open to judgment, to being found wanting. A work displayed means the most hidden parts of oneself—even one's awful anger—are revealed. The others may see how important they are to you; how very much loved; how very much hated. Best not to finish! "When something is finished," the melancholy painter Arshile Gorky said, "that means it's dead, doesn't it? I believe in everlastingness. I never finish a painting—I just stop working on it for a while. The thing to do is always to keep starting to paint." One thinks of Virginia Woolf, so immensely vulnerable to criticism, and her name wraps a shroud about itself. Rather than suffer another attack of depression, she killed herself.

Freud's great essay on depression, "Mourning and Melancholia," begins in wonder at such black events. How, given our great self-love, is it *ever* possible to commit suicide? Why, Freud asked himself, does the melancholic call himself ugly when he is handsome, stupid when he is smart, savagely berate himself even to the point of killing himself? His accusations against himself are, Freud writes, contrary to all sense, be-

cause, really, they don't apply to *him*. It is the one he has lost
that he truly disparages, the beloved who left. The melancholic has taken the lost beloved within himself; he has, in
part, become the beloved. He attacks the beloved-within-him-
self, even kills himself, as a way of destroying the love object.
Such suicides, in Freud's view, are murders. Melancholia is a
mighty black dog, tearing in confusion at its own viscera.

And the alternative, the task? I began to learn that from
Rilke's great poem "Turning Point" (as translated by Stephen
Mitchell). Here, like the melancholic, the poet takes the world
into himself. He *looks,* and each time he looks, he imprints
within, as a part of himself, all that he saw. "Animals trusted
him, stepped/into his open look, grazing,/ . . . And the rumor
that there was someone/ who knew how to look,/ stirred
those less/ visible creatures:/ stirred the women." But the
world, finally, judges this looker. Painfully alone, in a hotel
bedroom, the voices of all that he has taken into himself
discuss "his heart, which could still be felt;/ debated what
through the painfully buried body/ could somehow be felt—
his heart;/ debated and passed their judgment:/ that it did not
have love." For merely to look, to imprint the world within
oneself as the melancholic lover does the beloved, isn't
enough. The lost beloved languishes inside one. More than
languishes, she is punished, for one berates her for having left.
So the world turns away from the looker. "(And denied him
further communions.)/ For there is a boundary to looking./
And the world that is looked at so deeply/ wants to flourish
in love." The looker is called to another task, and his very gifts
will, as in a fairy tale, become a curse to him unless he takes
up his task. Which is, Rilke says, to return the beloved—all
that is truly seen—with a different, wider life, in his art. In this
"heart-work" even the anger one felt at her can now be used

for her, in the angry, difficult strain of making, of giving birth, giving form—the exact words that cut and form the flesh of the image. So one returns what was seen, loved, lost—and so pressed within one—to the world. "Work of the eyes is done, now/ go and do heart-work/ on all the images imprisoned within you; for you/ overpowered them: but even now you don't know them./ Learn, inner man, to look on your inner woman,/ the one attained from a thousand/ natures, the merely attained but/ not yet beloved form."

Why, I wondered, does Rilke speak so authoritatively of an inner woman? Perhaps it's because the first loved object lost was, for all of us, our mothers, and each new loved object is the mother—almost, almost—refound. So each new loss, each turning away, becomes intertwined (for men and women both) with that first loss, and so with the feminine within each of us. In depression, one might say, the masculine, the imagined father, as bearer of morality in the form of judgment, disparages the sensual, the feminine, the mother-within. No wonder the depressive's moral argument with himself seems so horrifyingly familiar, even comfy: It is a scene around the family dinner table. So the depressive's question, "How can I stop mourning, stop punishing myself?" becomes: "How can I give birth to my mother?" (Of course, it is our mother, in memory, and as the very structure of our psyche, who holds us as we give birth to our mother!)

For me, one great embodiment of this story is the life of the painter Arshile Gorky, who struggled from 1926 to 1936 to reproduce in paint a small photograph of his mother and himself, as a boy. Each drawing and canvas of this series bears marks of the difficulty and importance of this task.

Gorky—whose given name was Vosdanik Manuk Adoian

—chose his first name from the Caucasian form of the Armenian "Arshak," which translates as Achilles. This name
reflected his melancholic disposition, and, I think, a special
relation to his mother, who, like Achilles', had granted both
a great power and a great flaw. Gorky and his mother, Lady
Shushanik, had been abandoned by his father and his sisters
in 1916, when they fled the destruction of Armenia. Lady
Shushanik, Gorky, and his younger sister Vartoosh,
remained, with little food or money. In 1918, when Gorky
was fifteen, Lady Shushanik died of starvation in her son's
arms.

Gorky and his younger sister made their way to Watertown,
Massachusetts. In America, Harold Rosenberg writes, Gorky
"took shelter in art from the strange continent upon which he
had been cast." Art became his world elsewhere within this
big, accusatory world, this nearly infinite empty space. His
studio was filled with paints, brushes, drawing papers, bolts of
canvas, "as if he intended to hole up there for a siege."

But the paintings of Gorky's long apprentice years in Massachusetts and New York were mediocre. Melancholiacs, in
their weakness, tend to idealize their parents, feeling always
a special need for their protection. (Such parents must be gods,
requiring, and worth, our adoration.) For Gorky this meant
finding the "protection of a master" for each of his paintings,
doing them in the style of Cézanne, or Picasso, or Miró. But
the protection of the parent, or the master, is also a way not
quite to declare oneself.

Gorky just begins to come out of hiding with the paintings—none of them ever quite finished—of himself and his
mother, canvases based on a small photograph saved back
from the destruction of Armenia, of his family, of his childhood. This photo, probably from a neighborhood portrait

shop, shows Lady Shushanik, seated, looking out full face, almost a little coldly. She is attended by her eight-year-old son, who stands a little apart from her, holding flowers, as if they were an offering.

Gorky—not yet ready to let the photo be reborn through him—made very few changes in transforming the photo into his paintings, only shifting a column in the photo's artificial backdrop, and giving a turn to the boy's right foot. Gorky apparently saw *faithfulness* to the photograph as his task, even, at one point, making the kind of grid amateur artists use, and copying the photo on to canvas square by square. I think there is an element of fear in such devotion—combined with the guilt of the survivor—as if Gorky feared what he might reveal of his own attitude to his subject if he deviated from the photo. (One feels this repressed anger, too, in the work of photo-realists, whose large machine-like copies of "reality" call attention to a monstrous world that repels human affection, that transforms us into mechanical slaves, capable only of copies. An inner or an outer world that we cannot truly transform we are bound to hate.) Gorky's "master" here, protecting him from self-declaration, is photography, or, really—as there is no neutral mechanical reality—whoever aimed the camera in that neighborhood flash studio. But heart-work requires some freedom—that the mother be reborn in and through you, not as a photo would have her, but as you alone can bear her. So Gorky couldn't finish the painting, couldn't get it right.

The canvas, even in the texture of the paint, gives a full account of his failed attempts. In all versions of the painting Gorky's technique is exact, painstaking. At several stages on each canvas, Gorky has let the paint dry, then scraped the surface with a razor blade until it was smooth. He wiped away all excess paint and dust with a damp cloth and painted again. By the time he abandoned the canvas he had a picture thick with paint that hardly showed brush strokes. He had effaced his own hand, disguising his own involvement in producing the image. By this technique Gorky tried instantly to give the canvas the look of an old master. Gorky's surface, William Seitz writes, has "the soft glow of old marble or porcelain," with the effect of emphasizing "the hieratic dignity and mask-like intentness of the mother's face." Lady Shushanik becomes an icon, an adored Saint, though in that masklike quality, some sense of her indifference, and Gorky's unacknowledged anger, may show through. Gorky intuits, I think, that his task is to let his mother, in himself, be reborn as his creation, but he still cheats his fate. The composition is the photographer's, the texture is that of old masters, or the monastery's devotional object.

Gorky will not yet bear his mother. But these paintings mark the beginning of the process by which he will become himself. He required one more phase of discipleship—to surrealism—which allowed him a freer communication with his buried childhood, its store of lost objects mixed with the feminine in himself. (Gorky, for example, identified his mother's butterchurn as the basis of the bootlike object in so many of his later paintings.) Now he allowed his hand to move as it would, free associating, bringing up the past in his own manner. But this begins, Harold Rosenberg writes, in Gorky's regard for facts in these portraits of himself and his mother. One must add, he had also to learn *the proper regard for facts,* that facts must be mixed with one's own lifeblood, the images no longer distorted by the denigration of the feminine-within, or petrified by adoration—which are faces of the same coin. Still, these portraits, in their failed attempt to discover the facts not of "reality" but of memory, form the link, as Rosenberg says, to Gorky's great paintings, such as the 1944 *How My Mother's Embroidered Apron Unfolds in My Life.*

But one's fate is also made under conditions the world gives. In a 1948 auto accident Gorky broke his neck and paralyzed his painting arm. In July his wife, Agnes, left with their children. This was a loss that he could not overcome through painting, nor could he make good the loss of the ability to paint. On July 21, he committed suicide.

The figure of a melancholic artist unhappily pinned to a photograph reminds me of Delmore Schwartz's great story "In Dreams Begin Responsibilities." Here the unnamed narrator (whom I will call Delmore) enters a movie theater, and finds the feature already in progress. It is the story of his father's courtship of his mother! His eyes fixed on the screen—for what child wouldn't be fascinated by this primal scene—he sinks into his seat, into the soft darkness. "I am anonymous, and I have forgotten myself. It is always so when one goes to the movies, it is, as they say, a drug." Schwartz's metaphor of a film for the depressive's untransformed memory has a decisive brilliance. It teaches us that if one does not acknowledge and overcome one's angry fascination with one's internalized parents, then one will unconsciously project them outward on to everyone one encounters. Projection of a scene isn't heart-work, any more than copying a photograph is. Schwartz's mechanical metaphor is strikingly appropriate, for in unconscious projection one doesn't acknowledge that it is oneself who forms the pictures, making the world a screen for the unclaimed images of one's past. And one always projects what one unconsciously disparages, and what one will continue to disparage then, as if it were the world. So one remains excluded from life, watching shadows, as if in the womb of Plato's cave, or Loew's theater.

Delmore's parents-to-be meet in his grandparents' house, and his father makes small talk with his mother's parents. Uneasy, Delmore's father grows gruff with his mother, and this makes his grandfather rub his bearded cheek with worry. Is this man a suitable match for his daughter? This concern stops the film. *Will they marry? Will Delmore be born?* But as "my mother giggles at my father's words, the darkness drowns me." She giggles; they will marry; he will be born. (Or will he, really?)

In any case, for the moment Delmore draws the womb-like warmth of the theater around him, and watches his parents stroll on a boardwalk by the sea. She relates the plot of a novel she's been reading, and "my father utters judgments of the characters as the plot is made clear to him. This is a habit which he very much enjoys, for he feels the utmost superiority and confidence when he approves and condemns the behavior of other people." Delmore's father's relation to his wife and his world is impatient, judgmental, disparaging. All this Delmore has learned, for his relation to what he watches is also that of judge. (Of course, art requires some morality, some themes, just as it requires sensuousness and detail. But such themes aren't judgments; they're closer to the shape of questions than the steel of completed arguments. And in a work of art, that lovely hermaphroditic animal, that perfect marriage of masculine and feminine, one can't always tell which is which, what is form, what content, what is detail and what is theme.)

As Delmore's parents stroll, his father boasts, exaggerating the amount of money he earned in the week, though it "need not have been exaggerated. But my father has always felt that actualities somehow fall short." Delmore begins to weep, disturbing the other patrons. Should they marry, should he be born? One is reminded of Heine's melancholic poem (translated by Robert Lowell): "sleep is lovely, death is better still/ not to have been born is of course the miracle." This false possibility haunts the melancholic's life, and the lives of those who love him. Consciously or unconsciously, he confronts himself with it over and over, as a form of self-punishment, a painless suicide. But his constant meditation on this false choice is itself the suicide; by it, he remains outside life in his melancholy; not born; not living; not dead. As if watching a movie!

His parents stroll, go on a merry-go-round, have an expensive dinner. His father, carried along by his sense of well-being, surprises himself by proposing. Delmore tries to perform "the miracle," and choose not having been born. " 'Don't do it,' " he shouts at the screen. " 'It's not too late to change your minds, both of you. Nothing good will come of it, only remorse, hatred, scandal, and two children whose characters are monstrous.' "

An usher quiets Delmore, and his parents walk on, stopping at a booth to have their photo taken, and it is, no doubt, just the sort of studio where Gorky and his mother had their picture done. Why this repetition? Perhaps because until the heart-work is performed the memories of our childhood are just kitsch, badly staged, with false backdrops. Photos like that attempt to cheat death, as if there could be moments outside time, outside the narrative that we ourselves must not only suffer but will, even as it effaces us and the people we love. Photos remain kitsch until we make them into elements of the consciously told story of our lives, aware of ourselves telling the story in anger and in love, showing the power of death in the laws and limits of form, and in the ongoing rush of the narrative.

Delmore's father becomes impatient with the photographer: " 'Come on, you've had enough time, we're not going to wait any longer.' " The unsatisfactory picture is taken. They walk on, and his mother wants to go to a fortune teller. His father disapproves. "And then, in terrible anger, my father lets go of my mother's arm and strides out, leaving my mother stunned . . . and [I] begin to shout once more. . . ." Will she follow him? " 'What are they doing?' " Delmore shouts at the screen. " 'Don't they know what they are doing?' . . . [T]he usher has seized my arm and is dragging me away, and as he does so, he says, 'Why don't you *think* of what you're doing? [E]very-thing you do matters too much.' " Delmore is cast out into the sun of his twenty-first birthday. Birthday? But will Delmore ever be fully born, seeing this movie through to the end, *and then truly retelling it himself, as his own story?* Or will he continue to project his fate, rather than bearing it? In any case, Delmore Schwartz, the writer, has given us a profound and beautiful metaphor for this quandary, in a story of stunning directness. Even the overwrought self-pity and self-hatred of the narrator succeed as elements of his tangle, showing the forces that must be transformed, used as the anger of making, if he is not to remain enthralled. The task is here at least begun in this naming of the task.

" '. . . [E]verything you do matters too much.' " I hear in this an echo of moral "chosenness," that knife edge hyperbole which aggrandizes, and terrifies. Allen Dow, the perhaps semi-autobiographical character in one of John Updike's most moving stories, "Flight," counts the cost of this defense against depression. Allen is, one might say, enthralled to hyperbole. Without it, like many depressives, and most teen-agers, he feels inadequate. "At the age of seventeen I was poorly dressed and funny-looking, and went around thinking about myself in the third person. 'Allen Dow strode down the street and home.' . . . Consciousness of a special destiny made me both arrogant and shy."

Allen has been granted his special destiny by his mother, herself a master of hyperbole. "[M]y mother's genius was to give the people closest to her mythic immensity. I was the phoenix. My father and grandmother were legendary invader-saints . . . both of them serving and enslaving their mates. . . . For my mother felt that she and her father alike had been destroyed by marriage. . . ." Allen's mother takes him to a hill-top to show him their small town, Olinger, the site of so much of Updike's best work. "Suddenly she dug her fingers into the hair on my head and announced, 'There we all are, and there we'll all be forever. . . . Except you, Allen. You're going to fly.' . . . [I]t felt like the clue I had been waiting all my childhood for. My most secret self had been made to respond. . . ."

Allen's gift for flight most definitely includes his own talent for hyperbole, a way of *making things interesting.* For as all writers know, actualities fall short. We require the glow that transference gives in our loves, and the spice of myth in our stories. But the writer must learn the technique of hyperbole, not drug himself with it, for a novel that is all hyperbole, like the work of Anaïs Nin, say, is, in this secular age, unconvinc-ing, too unironic. Human gods are, after all, unreliable as sources of chosenness. Allen's mother is "impulsive and ro-mantic and inconsistent. I was never able to develop this spurt of reassurance into a steady theme between us. . . . 'You'll never learn, you'll stick and die in the dirt just like I'm doing. Why should you be better than your mother?' " For a parent often wants a child to fly beyond her, but hates it when he seems about to leave her—earthbound, aging, mortal. So the young aviator feels worthless if he fails, and grieves if he succeeds. Perhaps this accounts for the melancholy that haunts those who have gone beyond their parents, the sadness of immigrants and their children, of progress, of America.

Allen must redeem all that his implacable mother has suffered, "the inheritance of frustration and folly that had descended from my grandfather to my mother to me, . . . that I, with a few beats of my grown wings, was destined to reverse and redeem." If he does not, she will withdraw his special fate—a chosenness that also allows him, barely, to withstand the black mass of suffering, the family history that she has transmitted, and that he must redeem. The power to realize his ambition and the necessity for it both come from his mother.

In "Flight," Allen fails his mother by loving a high-school girl that she finds ordinary. "Don't go with little women, Allen. It puts you too close to the ground." Allen, too, disparages Molly even as he describes her. "Except for a double chin, and a mouth too large and thick, she would have been perfectly pretty in a little woman's compact and cocky way." Yet when he is with her, Allen can be a self rather than strut the one that, like an ill-fitting suit, has been given him by another. With Molly, he doesn't have to think of himself in the third person; she does not require that he be a messiah. "We never made love in the final, coital sense," but "she gave herself to me anyway, and I had her anyway, and have her still, for the longer I travel in a direction I could not have taken with her, the more clearly she seems the one person who loved me without advantage. I was a homely, comically ambitious hillbilly. . . ."

Which woman—which sense of himself—shall he choose? He vacillates. "Every time I saw my mother cry, it seemed I had to make Molly cry. Even in the heart of intimacy, half-naked each of us, I would say something to humiliate her. . . ." But there can be no real contest. He needs his mother's mythologizing to certify that he is special, and so protect him from that equally strong voice that says he is nothing, that he will stick in the dirt. Requiring her hyperbole as a drug against her sadness, he is a slave to her. Enslaved, how can he not be enraged by the feminine, and—as he so often does—denigrate it?

Which is to say, can Updike give birth to Olinger, to the feminine, without too much of the spice of hyperbole—like Gorky's overdone adoration—or the mud of denigration? He must bear his mother, and all that is bound up with her, not as projection, but as artistic creation, not as something alien—as sometimes Updike's female characters seem—but as something one is connected to, has participated in giving birth to, like so much of the beautifully realized world in his work, the lovely multifoliate details.

In the final confrontation Allen's mother requires a choice, a sacrifice. " 'Why do you torment the girl?' "

" 'To please you.' "

" '. . . It may be. I forget, you were born here.' "

"In a dry tone of certainty and dislike—how hard my heart had become—I told her, 'All right. You'll win this one, Mother; but it'll be the last one you'll win.'

"My pang of fright following this . . . seemed to blot my senses. . . . In a husky voice that seemed to come across a great distance, my mother said, with typical melodrama, 'Goodbye, Allen.' "

If Allen is to be free of her, then this must be an almost unmythologized story. Yet his mother is *prodigiously* good at mythologizing. The ending, one might say, shows a slight umbilical cord still (his mother not quite born) in its sentimentality, the words skewed by bearing more feeling than they can ever earn in others' eyes. Still, this gives a charming air of the ridiculous to the story's conclusion, all the unseen importance that family fights have, that Updike knows so well: "As if each generation of parents commits atrocities against their children which by God's decree remain invisible to the rest of the world."

I think then, finally, in wonder, of the great genius and great good fortune of Isaac Babel, who was able to use the feminine not to disparage, but to gain, the feminine. In one of the most charming of stories, "Reply to an Inquiry," Babel recounts how he at once became a writer, and lost—or overcame—his virginity, during his first visit to a prostitute, named Vera. "Every evening she emerged in Golovinsky prospect and, tall and white faced, glided before the throng like the figurehead of the Virgin Mary on the fishing boats. I stole after her, speechless. I saved money, and at last summoned the necessary courage."

That evening in bed, they begin to chat. " 'Why do you sit there so downhearted like?' she asked, drawing me toward her. '. . . . Are you a thief?'

" 'No, I'm not a thief, I'm a boy . . .'

" 'I can see you're not a cow,' said Vera, yawning. She could hardly keep her eyes open."

So to keep Vera from turning away, he creates a story for

her, " 'A boy,' I repeated, 'a boy for the Armenians.' I turned cold at the suddenness of my own invention."

At fifteen, he continues, he became the lover of an Armenian named Stepan Ivanovich, attracted by his wealth—for Vera will appreciate that motive, and the young Babel has a melancholic's gift for feeling with others, for knowing what his audience wants. Then, when the Armenian lost his (imaginary) money, Babel, he says, left him for another rich man, a churchwarden. "This bit I stole from some writer—it was the invention of a lazy mind. . . . I began to blather about these people, about their roughness and greed—a lot of nonsense I had once heard. . . ." But the nonsense moves Vera. " 'Well, and have you had any women?' asked Vera, turning toward me.

" 'How should I? Who would let me go near them?' "

Then Babel tells us of his night with Vera, ". . . I will interrupt my story here to ask you, comrades, if you have ever seen a village carpenter building a house for one of his own trade. With what speed and strength and joy the shavings fly from the log he is planing!"

And, of course, from her fellow workman, Vera will not accept payment. " 'Want to fall out with me, little sister?' "

"No, I did not want to fall out with her. We agreed to meet that evening, and I put back in my purse my two gold pieces—the first money I ever earned for a story."

Freud somewhere says that the artist is able to use his daydreams to get fame, money, and love. He should have added that it is sometimes by giving birth to the mother within himself, the feminine world within himself, that the male (and perhaps the female) artist achieves these worthy goals.

Of course Vera, too, will someday turn away from Babel, and be pressed into him, to become him. There is always a new aspect of the beloved pressed into the self by the depressive, for the world, as it dies, slowly turns itself away from us; even our body, slowly effaced by time, abandons us; and to save the beloved world back, we make it part of our psyche. We must not turn against that inner world in anger for leaving us, but use that anger in our task, that the dying world might be reborn in our work.

ALMOST ONE

☐ The project of our modernity: *To start from nothing,* not before or after the transcendental, not in relation to it, and to create for ourselves, having grasped the lineaments of our being, a new humanity. Or so the project began. For the unmoored nature here described—from nothing! impossible!—is unbearable, perhaps unlivable, and leads, in Lawrence, in Pound, in Jung, and even, perhaps, in the austere atheist Freud, to a longing to greet the return of the gods.

Many parts of post-modernism seem like a comical version of this howdy-do—and they are the more useful, the more American, I think, for their comedy. For the modern project has more than a whiff of megalomania and oppression, of Those Who Know, forming, in reeducation camps and interrogation rooms, the new humanity. The modern project has come to grief in the violently whimsical re-creations of animals in the gene-splicing laboratories, in the Holocaust, in the atomic flash-boom, in the gulag. . . . Particularly, I think, the gulag. Not because the horror was greater—how could one calibrate such a thing?—rather because Marxism embodied for many the paradigmatic modern project of self-remaking.

In Marx's vision, we're made by others, or by an economic system so that the system might continue. (Marx doesn't much distinguish between what occupies a certain place in a system and a "person.") Workers would like some say in a making which now they can only suffer. Knowing that their self-making occurs only through the socially determined economic process, they will begin with each other, Marx thought, the collective dialogue to change their conditions and themselves.

Marx's errors are many, but for the moment I want to concentrate on this: that he thought that the personality was made by one realm only, saw us as a version of homo economicus, class creatures, made for and by the economy—and we may experience that making as a suffering. But we know that there is more to be included in our making than the economic. That *isn't* to say that the economic isn't part of what makes us, but we're also formed (for example) by irrational symbols, by fantasies. (Those fantasies may play a role in molding what is produced, like our "cigarette-shaped" boats, and the way it's produced, just as what we have produced may enter into, limit and shape, our fantasies.)

If you have no identity outside of one made by the process of production, if all other identities are false, imposed, ideological, then *who* will speak in this communal dialogue? (Or is all possibility already foreseen by that magisterial, authoritative entity, the Party, the voice of the class and its place in production? In which case the collective dialogue is a sham, its outcome already known by Those Who Know.) And who will *emerge* from this revolutionary dialogue? If the necessities of the economic system make us, how can one after the revolution be different from what one is now, a metaphor for a place in the process of production, a mouthpiece for the process? Marxism, and the modern project generally, never put much stress on the individual speaker, on what architects call "defensible personal space"—as one can see from the different names some modern thinkers have given to what they think *really* speaks in our collective dialogue: "the species essence"; "the will to power"; the "it." (Most of what we call "I," much of the self, is, to many modern thinkers, a fiction, and their ideas of our remaking often sound, to our contemporary ears anyway, like our disappearance.)

Many projects were bound up with the strand of modernism embodied by Marxism and were implicated in its failures. For Marxism's grand narrative and its institutions stood surety, whether acknowledged or not, for many other contiguous efforts, in much the same way that many branches of therapy relate to the narrative and institutions of psychoanalysis. One by now conventional sign for the failure of this modernism is the "unlivability" of modernist housing, like the blocks of housing at Pruitt Igoe in St. Louis that were so loathed they were simply destroyed. The project of remaking the self (through housing design, through social planning) was found to be unlivable (in somewhat the same way, I think, that *Finnegans Wake* is thought to be unreadable). In each case the project, its critics say, took leave of history, thought one could start from nothing and forget the needs history has shown we have—for characters and story in fiction, for "defensible personal space" in architecture.

One kind of post-modernism is an irony about the modern project's failure. The modern is retained as material from which "building techniques" may be borrowed, "quotations" can be made. This makes the modern a moment in the history of style, and as that the modern becomes a joke on itself, unaware, so to speak, that it has already failed, and its failure shown by the way that it can be used as "quotation." For if the modern can be quoted, it didn't put an end to the pre-history of mankind, didn't inaugurate its own proper dissolution-continuation in a permanent revolution that would continue its project. Modernism becomes another episode not in the history of our self-making, but in the pageant of style, the self's adornment. In itself, cut off from other systems of explanation, style can't account for its own transformations; it has no history, just a record, and no motive for its changes but boredom. The other systems of explanation—which might show what makes a style, or what causes boredom—would rejoin us with questions about why we take *this* shape, have *these* tastes. Much post-modernism is anxious to prevent that move, seems content with history as a pattern-book of styles, offering samples we can romp among.

Often the post-modernist architect takes several fragments from the pattern-book and places a quotation from the modern *against* what he or she calls the vernacular, as if the slang phrase, the Las Vegas neon fantasy, or the hand-made roadside sign showed an inevitable human nature that modernism had ignored and which now, like the repressed, has returned. Human nature as the *resistance* to remaking, the resistance to modern history, is represented by the neighborhood architecture, the Las Vegas neon fantasy that is mimicked in the post-modern building. I think this is a misunderstanding of the vernacular and somewhat of a con, even if, as with Michael Graves's chirping tea kettle, often a charming one. The mere quotation of slang usually disguises, or half-disguises, or just attempts to make comfy, the actual work of the world, which has already turned much of the hand-made world, too, into a relic, another material for quotation. So the quote from the vernacular that adorns the top of the AT&T corporate headquarters may say that there are limits to the control exercised by capitalism, limits in the ever-present needs and the resistance to transformation represented by the vernacular quotation, but, in truth, and willy-nilly, the capitalist transformation proceeds apace. And it, too, is a remaking of the self, though one, like the communist project, bureaucratically rather than democratically controlled. (That the best laid corporate marketing plans sometimes go awry doesn't mean that a plan wasn't made, power wasn't exercised—even if from a few competing power centers—factories moved, cities destroyed, workers relocated, retrained, re-formed.)

And yet, there's a lot one can learn from post-modernism, too. For, of course, there was no starting from nothing. We're made up of other discourses, fragments, quotations, words already spoken, however transvalued we might want to make those words. History does indicate a reckoning we must make with needs that must be met. The modernist critique may have discovered that the *need* is for a *fiction,* as for example, the collective fiction of the self. But that doesn't make the self *non-existent*—for we have still found it necessary to act *as if* the self exists, and perhaps we always will require the fiction of contracts, signatures, Valentine's Day cards. (*I* love you. Do *you* love me?) Upon such legal fictions, legality may depend; and woe to the world without such ties of obligation and limit!

In any case, intellectual nihilism—seeing through everything—can be bitter food for people who find themselves none the less trapped within a restrictive world that won't go away simply because it's been seen through. When feminists, blacks, gays, among others, took up the tools of modern theory with their pressing needs, they found (and made) something useful there that went beyond critique, that reshouldered the positive part of the modern project with a post-modern twist. For if the self, and culture, are as post-modernism teaches *necessary* fictions, they are still "fictions": and so can also be retold. Perhaps we can tell a better story that creates a better self (and one that knows its provisional nature as well as its necessity).

I think that post-modernism, in its turn to vernacular art, understood, too, where the important lessons were to be learned about *how* to re-form our fictions. But I think we need to understand what animates the vernacular rather than simply quoting from it. Appreciative critics of post-modernism are right, I think, when they identify some aspects of the post-modern—like Portman's Hyatt towers, or Warhol's *Diamond Dust Shoes*—with fancy. But beyond the pleasures of fancy there is the realm of the imagination, where quotations were gathered by the vernacular artist, and respoken, not to make an ironic comment on the past, but in order to re-imagine the new. So in turning to the vernacular artist, we need to discover how to continue *his* project—for the vernacular artist embodied more than an ironic resistance to the modern, and provided more than the satisfaction of a need unmet by the modern. Like the "high" modernists, he or she, too, was striving to remake a self—this time, not from nothing, but from already given elements.

Vernacular art isn't just the demotic; it was always the joining of the demotic phrase with the "high-toned"; it's embodied in the title of The Erskine Hawkins Orchestra's tune:

"Tuxedo Junction," or the way Art Tatum provides a Whitmanesque world of inclusion when he plays Massenet (and when he plays practically anything else, too). Nor is it just such high-low conjunctions, for jazz isn't just art about classes; it says the difficult words en masse and contains multitudes: train sounds, the hard beat of the work world, the repeated curses of the assembly line worker, the gaudy dress of the honky-tonk queen. (Let the varied beauty and sophistication of the blues represent the demotic; then the jazz musician is the vernacular artist, culling his materials from all over, joining them to the blues. Or let the blues musician represent the vernacular artist, transforming the field holler by joining it to the adumbrations of modern industry, the dislocations of a decaying and savage feudalism.)

Joining realms together can lead to irony, as in postmodernism, thus cancelling meanings, or it can reveal new resources of meaning in each realm. It can save the style of the high art from pomposity, and show the demotic phrase to have potencies different from vulgarity—ones that look good in a tuxedo. When such works fail it may be because one realm condescends, not realizing the severity of the particular training that the vernacular art requires, as when the symphony plays jazz without having the training needed to give the living pulse of swing, or when an opera singer thinks she has the right to sing the blues. (She may, but again not have the life-education.) The joinings can be kitsch—as when many jazz musicians swing the classics. Or they can be the sort of post-modern architecture that mocks not the pretensions but the very deepest impulse of the modern and of the demotic by its deceptive linkages. Tone and attitude are crucial, there is mockery that is ugly and angry, and some that tells lies—as if the new corporate headquarters with its filigreed headpiece were really just a local grocery store hypertrophied.

But there's mockery, too, that allows the demotic and the high art phrases to recognize what they have in common, something *not known* before the joining. (Maybe that's the American way of representing what Marx calls our "species essence.") This sort of mockery is described by the great vernacular artist Ralph Ellison in his tribute to Duke Ellington. Ellington's speech and his music could be

> as mocking of our double standards, hypocrisies, and pretensions as the dancing of those slaves who . . . imitated the steps so gravely performed by the masters . . . and then added to them their own special flair, burlesquing the white folks and then going on to force the steps into a choreography uniquely their own. . . . [A] European cultural form was becoming Americanized, undergoing a metamorphosis through the mocking activity of a people partially sprung from Africa. So, blissfully unaware, the whites laughed while the blacks danced out their mocking reply.

These mocking *yet beautiful* joinings have produced our greatest American music, and this kind of democratic vernacular technique has also given us some of our finest novels, starting with our great progenitor, that strong cable made of many languages roughly braided, *Moby Dick*. (Melville's novel gathers many genres, too: plays, scientific treatises, poems, songs, adventure tales, etymologies. Each represents a different embodiment for the character and the story; a full portrait requires a panoply of ways of telling.) After

Ahab's bold nervous lofty language, *Huckleberry Finn* transforms valorous heroism by joining it to the demotic, inventing the slangy rebellion of youth (the juvenile delinquent, the campus activist). And Zora Neale Hurston's *Their Eyes Were Watching God* makes bitter-sweet conjunctions of romantic rhetoric and richly stylized Afro-American rural talk; together they open into new possibilities of elegant sensuous apprehension.

I think that jazz may point the way forward for the postmodern because, for artists who don't want to ignore the contributions of modern theory, jazz shows the possibilities of an art at once sensuous and *abstract.* Another chorus from Ralph Ellison: The Afro-American (he told James McPherson)

... can't even trace our blood back only to Africa because most of us are part Indian, Spanish, Irish, part any every damn thing.... [C]*ulturally*] we represent a synthesis of any number of these elements. And that's a problem of abstraction in itself; it's abstraction and recombining. ... When we began to build up a sense of ourselves, we did it by abstracting from the Bible, abstracting the myths of the ancient Jews, the early Christians, modifying them as we identified with these people, and projecting ourselves. This was an abstract process ... a creative process, one of the most wonderful things which ever happened on the face of the earth, the *re-unification* of a shattered group of people. ... Now, American Negro music was not simply the product of remembered African rhythms. ... The jig and the flings which the Irish and the Scots had brought over from the British Isles were appropriated by the slaves and combined with African dance patterns. And out of this abstraction and recombination you got the basis of the American choreography.

Vernacular art is abstract (or one might say, *theoretical*), as in the way jazz uses theory to look to the deep structure of the tunes that it plays, the chords, for example—here called "changes"—and makes them the ground of new possibilities, new tunes. Jazz models that longed-for beautiful conversation, the beloved community, in which each player tries to determine the ground of his self-creation, the collective conditions that make him, and that make him now under conditions that he can only suffer. (It all must be found by the player in the music; even the way the tune, the "standard," was first bought and sold; its residual beauty, its sentimental deceit tell him something of how he is made.) Here he can recognize those conditions; enter into them and make modest but crucial alterations; model their transformation into song.

In the post-modern novel now (but I'd prefer to call it the *modern* post-modern novel), the languages to be joined are ones that have, as in jazz, undergone an abstraction, a theoretical examination. The discourses of our many pursuits (as lovers and as businesswomen, as members of a tribe or a race, as patriarchs and as gendered animals) are scrutinized till they reveal how they give a self. Only those realms truly have "a theory" to contribute that produce a credible—if partial—self, a little misshapen golem, a homunculus that still manages to move.

Theory is part of that modern self-scrutiny which specialization made possible, when for mastery, to increase efficiency, we parceled realms, and then tried to puzzle out how each divided realm operated. But blinded by the specialization that allows for their insight, each specialist may feel that his theory (about sexuality, about gender, about signs, about power and history) has recorded how *the* self is created. This leads to fantastical and sometimes self-righteous assertions. (It is work for aesthetics, and for the moral imagination, to chasten this hyperbole.)

Any post-modern-yet-still-modern work contains some of the many discourses that create a subject. (I have in mind novels by—among others—Toni Morrison, John Barth, Thomas Pynchon.) The novelist, of course, doesn't simply describe, but shows each realm in the process of producing a *partial* self. He or she may first imagine the character produced by the job he performs and the consciousness it shapes—the self it gives. But that is not a satisfying full existence in either life or art; the maimed creature cries out for more, to be fed, to be made fuller. (There's a recurrent question asked of literary theory: If the self is a fiction, then who writes? Perhaps the answer is that *responsiveness* writes. Need calls out, and we provide food to fill that need, as if we can't help ourselves, for we each wish to eat and to be eaten, to be filled and to provide food for others.) So the writer replies to his maimed creature, and adds the character's fantasies, and his bodily apprehensions, his historical situation; his theology; his fundamental metaphysical predicaments. Each language, which is to say each aspect of our separated specialized lives, leaves something out, gives us, for the time we must occupy that language, that role, only a partial person. Only when they can be unified will we create, for our age of specialization, the rounded characters that Forster describes in *Aspects of the Novel,* or have that "even-sided" development that Marx dreamed of (even as he, undone by his specialization, mistook us for economically produced creatures only).

In Thomas Pynchon's *Gravity's Rainbow,* for example, character is formed by the joining of the discourses of sexuality and fantasy and politics and technology and media. I think there is, in contrast to many earlier novels, sometimes a coldness and an attenuation in his modern-post-modern characters. That coldness comes, in part, because the novel tracks not the education of a character, but the work of the world by which a character is made to be educated; the ways a self is made, not the amours of an already made self with which we might identify. And the feeling of attenuation may come because the wider sense of self can only result from a joining of languages, and so a character can't have much density until the narrative is well under way, and only if it is all held in mind at once—for the narrative *is* the joinings that gives the substantial self, as the partial person quests for new roles to fill, different embodiments, a fuller self.

The question of *Gravity's Rainbow* might be phrased as: Will we allow this making to be done by "they," or can it be taken back and reshaped, as this novel itself does, to reveal that machinery, and to intimate, as well, the fresh beauties available to us from new conjunctions? Pynchon's genius is not only in the number of languages, scientific and historic and slangy, that he joins, but in this two-edged statement—a rejoining which shows (sometimes within one loping brilliantly articulated sentence) the diabolical (but hidden) machinery already in place and making us up, and the ways we might rework the pieces to other ends.

The novel experiments with how the different languages—taken back to ground, to where subjects are given—can be joined; it tests if their joinings can be lived as a narrative, as a coherent life; *if* they make a world. And the novel shows, too, where the languages fail to meet but might; or, alas, can never meet. (There are many bridges across our divisions in Pynchon's work, for example, that just chute-the-chute you into the ocean.) There are needs within history—for personal coherence, for a deeper implication in each other's lives—but it's through the stories we *can* tell (and we can't tell just any story) that we learn what joinings they will permit. Our "nature" (like our character) isn't known until the story's told.

The vernacular project embodies, I think, the kinds of dreaming required by democracy. The way we form our personality, and the way we participate in making our American nation, both come from a gathering and recombining of languages. Democratic citizens are vernacular artists, each imagining how to braid up our nation's scattered, partial selves into a wider national identity. Out of these many voices music might come—as is demonstrated in jazz polyphony (which from the first has included spirituals, and Latin-American music, and jigs). Think of the player at work in a collective improvisation and you have the image of the American citizen who might speak in the democratic dialogue, making himself and participating in the formation of his community—when we fully give democracy a try. In the call-and-response form so basic to Afro-American music one shouts out one's need, and so asks for a response. The improvisation is democratically open-ended because when the other speaks to feed you, he also states his need, pleads for your reply. You must respond to the other voices, for they are, in part, what make you, and what you must chime with if music is to be made. So we citizen-players, each in our own minds, form an image of the giant (the nation, the collective, the music, the narrative, the novel), but our image differs from what we want to hear, it needs something: the notes that we are called on to play, to repair the whole. But our notes, too, unknowingly carry within themselves a void, a need, and it must be responded to. . . .

So one learns new discourses and the partial subjects they give in order to gather them into a novel or a nation. Out of many one—our national motto. Or *almost one:* For our need, too, is contained in the word we add, and it requires a reply, and so the national improvisation will go on, let us hope, forever, as we each help to form, out of many, almost one. (It's from being off-balance that we get that swing.)

LOOKING

HIGH AND LOW

☐ *Krazy Kat,* the comic strip whose career ran from 1913 to 1944, was, during most of its working life, immensely popular, often holding top banana position on the comics page. But, in her last decade, when Krazy lost some of her following—except for a devoted coterie that fortunately included her boss, William Randolph Hearst—many newspapers transferred her to their cultural suburbs, the arts page. But of course! De Kooning and Picasso acknowledged themselves as fans of the Kat and her co-workers, Ignatz Mouse and Offissa Pup. And one might add E. E. Cummings and Philip Guston to the list of her admirers.

Many who wish to defend America's popular arts suffer from the sort of hangover those names represent—as if only high culture figures could give the imprimatur that would dignify our daily pleasures. But often the real trade goes the other way: New possibilities for pleasure are discovered in popular culture, in areas not yet fully incorporated into the metropolis of work and "commodified" leisure; these discoveries are then exploited by "high" artists—stylized, remarketed with designer labels. Lautrec worked and reworked the commercial posters of Paris, advertisements for the bar concerts that were themselves places for the high and low in society and art to mix. Renoir recut the styles of women's clothing. And the wildly egotistical hip-hop defacement of New York subways has become gallery art. (One must give a tip of the Hatlo hat to those art historians—among them T. J. Clark, Tom Crow, and Adam Gopnick—who have, each in his own way, mapped these trade routes and shown that the way up is the way down.)

Do the high artists add something to our pleasure beyond a formal stylization—one not always appropriate, as on those usually sad occasions when "jazz rhythm meets the philharmonic"? (In any case, Krazy was already a very stylish Kat, and Louis Armstrong a very sophisticated musician.) Or do the high culture entrepreneurs, simply by transposing joy to a new locale, make it briefly threatening to a museum culture which thrives on history, on inherited meanings—a culture that makes pleasure into a curriculum subject?

In any case, I don't think Krazy meant to be *threatening*. She was, apparently, equally happy on either the arts page or in the Sunday funnies (and I'm sure she has enjoyed her shows at the Whitney Museum of American Art, and at the Pompidou Center). Her daily and Sunday work shows a steady increase in Herriman's mastery, a refinement of elements, a discovery of the basic (which is rarely a starting point!), and in Herriman's later years a more limited but powerful dry brush line. Throughout, the strip was drawn in a brilliantly economical way, kinetic, with cross-cross shadings that form surprising conjunctions, border designs that delight, and a wild style interplay of geometric and free-hand forms. The layout is jazzy, complex in organization, rhythmically rich, filled with difficulty and reward.

Still, Krazy had her motifs "picked-up"—not that they had fallen!—by Philip Guston and Oyvind Fahlstrom. And many critics have treated her work as a proto-surrealism, raw material awaiting its high art apotheosis. But the high art that *Krazy Kat* has most affinity with—though, for reasons I'll discuss, there are ways that I think her work is sometimes the more interesting—is the very American picture plane of Robert Rauschenberg and Jasper Johns, the frame that might contain anything, commingling and turned at every angle. "Herriman's fantasy," the critic Robert Warshow wrote, "can be free and relaxed, it can go its own way. What came into his head went down on the paper." This reminds me of Leo Steinberg's descriptions of Johns and Rauschenberg: "Rauschenberg's picture plane had to become a surface to which anything reachable-thinkable would adhere. . . . And it seemed at times that Rauschenberg's work surface stood for the mind itself—dump, reservoir, switching center, abundant with concrete references freely associated. . . ." Herriman's language, Warshow wrote, "is built up of scraps of sound and meaning, all the echoes that his mind contained. . . ." Similarly, the Rauschenberg picture plane, Steinberg writes, contains "the waste and detritus of communication—like radio transmission with interference; noise and meaning on the same wavelength, visually on the same flatbed plane." No fixed, fast frozen relations: *Krazy Kat*'s background is in continual flux, for as Warshow says, "Herriman felt no obligation either to keep the background still or to explain its mobility." The landscape might grow from rocks into mesas from frame to frame, and Krazy Kat and Ignatz Mouse walking up a mountainside may find themselves in a tree branch at the top. Some aficionados of Krazy have pointed out that this wasn't surrealism but new world realism, that that's pretty much how the rocks look as the light changes in Monument Valley (or as technology changes the rocks into real Arnel). And not just the background changed. That most foreground of facts, Krazy's gender, was also mobile: sometimes our heroine was a hero. Like America, *Krazy Kat* was freed for "pure play," Warshow thought, because it needn't "be dignified or 'significant.' " Similarly, Steinberg's description of the Rauschenberg picture, where "[u]p and down are as subtly confounded as positive-negative space or figure-ground differential. . . . This picture plane could look like some garbled conflation of controls system and cityscape, suggesting the ceaseless inflow of urban message, stimulus and impediment." Warshow underlines *Krazy Kat*'s corrosion of meaning, calling it "lumpen culture," which, he says, has "a certain purity and freshness." The Marx Brothers, also denizens of this purlieu, "spit on culture." They are popular with "middle class intellectuals, . . . because they express a blind and destructive disgust with society that the responsible man is compelled to suppress. . . ." In *Krazy Kat,* "a sweet-tempered fantasy," the gap between mass culture and respectable culture is manifested "not in an open rejection of society, but, more indirectly, in a complete disregard of the standards of respectable art."

Both Steinberg's and Warshow's descriptions remind me of another locale without distinctions of high and low, up and down: "The id of course," Freud writes, "knows no judgments of value: no good and evil, no morality. . . . it has no organization. . . . The logical laws of thought do not apply in the id, and this is true above all of the law of contradiction. . . ." Like the id, Herriman's audience was, Warshow thought, "completely out of touch with the concerns of the serious minded.

. . . Where no art is important, *Krazy Kat* is as real and important a work of art as any other—it is only supposed to divert its readers for two minutes at a time. . . ." But later additions to Freud's work reveal—as Krazy does more profoundly even than Rauschenberg—that the id *does* have reasons, though reason may not understand them and think the id completely out of touch with the ego's serious-minded concerns. The unconscious has an organization. Desire, *Krazy Kat* showed by the ways it brought about the plot's daily repetitions, is *structured,* and the ability to be truly diverting, the freedom to play, the refusal of ordinary cultural significances is not, as Warshow seems to think, such a simple gift. (Though it is indeed a great gift to make it *look* simple.) The popular artist must *earn* that freedom. The comic pages are littered with work that fails at this, strewn with satirical strips, socially well-meaning strips, and wise guy kittens that are just Bob Hope in a cat suit. Such work lives in an obsequious or ironic or court jester relationship with the given cultural meanings. *Krazy Kat* did not; it was a world elsewhere. "Krazy Kat," Warshow writes, is " 'pointless' and 'silly,' it comes from the peripheral world where the aims and pretensions of society are not regarded." But it's hard to maintain space on the periphery; the cooptation factory that forms meaning out of fancy is a strong one.

Like Krazy, Rauschenberg had to be strategic in order to free himself from hierarchical meanings: "When in the 1960's he worked with photographic transfers," Steinberg writes, "the images—each in itself illusionistic—kept interfering with one another; intimations of spatial meaning forever cancelling out to subside in a kind of optical noise." But it's Krazy's genius not only to have evaded the given "meanings," but to provide something more than noise, to move from ordinary to extraordinary language. For to be freed to play, to be freed from high-culture morality is not to be without significance. The evenly modulated, repeating four-four beat of jazz is made vibrant by its varied accents, and it don't mean a thing if it ain't got that swing. But, if it *does* have that swing, perhaps a new world of meanings may be opened.

I wouldn't dream of *deciphering* Krazy, but I would like to know more about how she keeps time. That research might begin with what does not change in *Krazy Kat*'s constant transformations: the plot. Krazy Kat loves Ignatz Mouse. Implacable Ignatz hates Krazy, and the mouse enjoys nothing more than launching a brick to Krazy's noggin. When he succeeds hearts and flowers bloom over the Kat's bean. Krazy thinks, in her inimitable patois, "Li'l Anjil!" (Her vocables mark Krazy as an immigrant. But from where? Perhaps from the nightland of Joyce's *Finnegans Wake.* Or perhaps, like my grandfather, from Russia.) Offissa Bull Pup, himself hopelessly in love with the Kat, arrests the Mouse and flings him in jail. From which, unreformed, he emerges the next day to throw another—yet somehow the same—brick. George Herriman, who had the honor of recording these doings, rang every possible change on this eternal triangle + brick. And then he added some impossible variations, in a sustained lyric improvisation that had the quality of a sublime delirium.

It is hard for critics, myself most certainly included, to say what that delirium means, what the popular arts are up to. In part that's because the language of criticism developed along with its high art objects, so it hasn't developed the nerve endings to perceive what popular artists are doing—seeing them, generally, as either proto or debased forms of the high arts, or simple allegories of the social. But a comic strip isn't a debased kind of literary narrative or a debased form of drawing. It's a . . . comic strip. Perhaps one aspect of the critic's difficulty comes from criticism's intimate involvement with history in all its facets, while the popular arts, often, are engaged in an ecstatic refusal of time. *Krazy Kat,* for example, resists the slow effacement of the subject within time—that gentle melancholy that Japanese criticism (or so many contemporary American short stories) identifies as the aesthetic mood. Krazy also resists being an exemplar of the magnificent heroic eruption which *organizes* time, making it BC or AD. *Krazy Kat* is a different kind of gadget. The strip somehow allowed for an enormous amount of fresh incident—the variations within the daily strip—yet it managed *not* to generate narrative. And the work remains engaging to the reader throughout its span, yet it did *not* lead to the unfolding or development of character. This is not simply because, as so often in comics, no character in the strip ages—Mutt and Jeff didn't age, but neither would a collection of their work hold one's interest for very long. *Krazy Kat* somehow defused the forces which *make* and mark time, engaged and restructured them at the most basic level, in order to stop time.

Perhaps this gadget's central motor is Krazy's recurrent dionysian gesture, her *affirmation* of the brick. What we do with pain is, of course, one facet of what we do with death, that "nihilating negativity" that hollows out the world, Hegel says, and makes time. That is, it is by our deferrals of death that we make our sense of time, that postponement of our going under (and being reborn!) at every moment. Krazy doesn't *suffer* the brick; or accept it; or transform it. She loves the brick, as she loves all existence. In Krazy's world fulfillment and pain are facets of the same mouse-led force, and it is affirmed. But the Pup, who embodies order, knows that the brick might be, *should* be, *pain*—for then Krazy might prefer him, the lawman. The Pup frustrates libido—or mice, anyway—long enough to provoke ingenuity (the twists and turns of our sexuality). So this gadget *includes* the jail, includes the law as part of its mechanism. Krazy, though, may know something that the Pup chooses to ignore: that at the most primal level any strong excitation is affirmed, for it generates sexuality.

So perhaps Krazy, on the comic page, runs along the margin of history, providing the saving grace that we would need to put a stop to history, to close the circle into "eternal recurrence." (What might she call it? Perhaps, "Eaturnall wreckonallsense.") *That* would be worth knowing, so here's another attempt to blueprint the gadget, this time from the point of view of our characters' psychologies: Ignatz Mouse *cannot* be the sadistic monster that he wishes to be: his brick pleases Krazy. *Because* of that he throws them again and again like a crying child who tries to break out of his mother's orbit, to perform just one action that isn't what Krazy has already desired, and so ordained. (Poor Mouse, he can't hurt Krazy, can't have one moment where he is really big!) And the Kat, conversely, never plays the goddess to him, never hurts him, for she is pleased by all he does. Once again Krazy refuses all those transference games that make history—the charade of god and slave, of follow the leader—and does it in such a way as to make her over-and-over machine work.

The child that Freud describes in *Beyond the Pleasure Principle* repeats the game of fort-da because if the game is well and truly played time stops for the player and eternity is born. But it's not because of her failure that the child repeats a really good game; it's because of success. In a good game, death— death as repetition (for we wish, Freud says, to *return* to the inorganic, to repeat that previous state of play)—is not deferred but immediately reincluded in existence. And the repetition shows, like the repeated plot in *Krazy Kat,* a life satisfied with itself, wanting the same again. Consider the brick: Krazy is a lover seeking an object long ago lost. Refinding the brick is the rediscovery of LOVE. (Love is always a repetition.) And Krazy is fixed on a traumatic moment—when life emerged from the rocks, from the brick—and desires it again and again because s/he wants to return, to die. Thus the repetition of the brick means DEATH. So surely in a gadget where love and death are *properly* joined repetition will be born (or reborn) as the seal of ecstasy—the brick!

Pleasure, popular artist Krazy Kat shows us—brick after brick—is not the single, irreducible, tragic event. Ecstasy's true home is in children's bedtime stories—read it again please!—in the mesh of quilts and needlepoints, in (however paltry its way) T.V. shows like "Dallas," and in sex—the lyric, Baudelaire wrote, of the crowd. Let's have the same again—the changing same. Our joy in listening to George tell Gracie to say goodnight—night after night—is a foretaste of a better life to come, a full, satisfied life that doesn't strive, but wills repetition, dying and instantly reborn at every moment. Ignatz's mighty brick, the repeat in Buck and Bubbles' tap step, the slowly withdrawn foot of the moon-walking break-dancer, the tune coming round again in a Coltrane solo, make time stop—almost, almost—and speak of that single, timeless instant, eternity. As Herriman wrote from the hospital, "No I didn't do all that work while I was laid away—it's old stuff they picked out of the morgue and used over again.—my junk is so much the same—y'could use it backwards or forwards—now, or then—and nobody would know the Difference—that's how come I fooled 'em for ten weeks—." Herriman's genius was to vary things enough so that the strip allowed for invention—and few minds have been more fertile—yet somehow keep things from changing too much. The missive/missile must arrive in a new way—dropped from a balloon, or shooting through a trench—yet still be Ignatz's brick. Things are turned at *almost* any angle, but come out the same in the end. That texture of repetition, of love and pain—*but which is which in this vital death?*—is what makes *Krazy Kat* so full of delight and so worth wondering at.

My description of *Krazy Kat* may remind one of the programmatic slogans of the post-modern: a consciousness that is polymorphous in style, resistant to meaning, unrelated to history. "This is a rich and creative movement, of the greatest aesthetic play and delight," the Marxist critic Frederick Jameson writes of the post-modern, "that can be perhaps most rapidly characterized . . . by two important features: . . . the falling away of the protopolitical vocation, . . . and the eclipse of all the affect (depth, anxiety, terror, the emotions of the monumental) that marked high modernism, and its replacement by . . . aesthetic play, a commitment to the surface, and to the *superficial. . . .*" But, again, Krazy's structured play is poised *against* history, not ignoring it, but refusing it. Krazy is *reborn* over and over. The post-modern, by contrast, often acts as if history—"the protopolitical vocation"—had simply ground to a halt.

The Marxist unriddling of history's disguises was to say that the ruling ideology presented cultural facts as inevitable truths of nature. You might even say that modern thought depends on oppositions like the one between the mythic (in which culture is seemingly embedded in nature, is inevitable as it is) and the disenchanted view. The modern subject is the *process* of unriddling, of seeing through. Freud rewrites the Oedipus myth, but he does not think he is putting an end to it. The psychoanalytic subject will always stand between the transference (the myth) and the analysis of the transference (the disenchanted view), conducting the constant passage from one realm to the other. The seasonal "death and rebirth" provided for in the ritual, myth-ruled world will become, for the subject created *in* analysis, the anxiety that erupts—and is worked through—now here, now there during the analysis interminable.

The post-modern ideological maneuver accepts the Marxist critique, and says that *all* is, indeed, culture. ("I tend to regard the tilt of the picture plane from vertical to horizontal," Steinberg writes, "as expressive of the most radical shift in the subject matter of art, the shift from nature to culture.") But culture—and I hardly mean to blame Rauschenberg or Johns for the ways other forces have used them—is then defined as so many forms of *entertainment.* Post-modern ideology makes politics into surface, into spectacle, into performance. (How is the Great Communicator doing today *as* communicator? How does Colonel North's full metal jacket *play* in middle America?) The post-modern, by folding all into (*on* to) the cultural as entertainment, offers the pleasures of life as surface, as flat image. Most of all, this "superficial" offers, as Jameson writes, the escape from anxiety, from terror, from, that is to say, an apprehension of death—not by reincorporating it into, and so transforming life, in some krazy way . . . but by simply changing the station. After all, how can an image die?

Krazy's art is challenged from two directions: How could she have continued (had Herriman lived, for no one else could have continued his work) when the state's machinery has offered a giant, terrifying, false substitute for her brick—a social and technological death, an absolute blackness—a substitute that might too easily be confused with her personal (potentially loved, if you have the genius) fragment of death-at-each-moment, the brick. "Tolstoy's enormous experience of Nature," Rilke wrote, "made him . . . able to think and write out of a sense of the whole, out of feeling for life which was permeated by the finest particles of death, the sense that death was contained everywhere in life, like a peculiar spice in life's powerful flavor. But that was precisely why this man could be so deeply, so frantically terrified when he realized that somewhere there was pure death, the bottle full of death . . . out of which people were forced to drink a bitterness of undiluted death." The brick is the spice; the bomb is the bottle full of death.

Our response to this is the post-modern fancy; we change the station. How then is our Kat to conduct her vaudeville when the margin she danced on has disappeared *as* margin? Politics has become entertainment, for who, now, could care ever to remember what politics *really* is (without, that is, becoming "frantically terrified")? The pleasures of the flat, the fanciful have become part of the design of the consumer's world, of the weightlessness of his choices, of history as choice of lifestyles. How can Krazy oppose her true fancy—won from the forces of striving, of profundity—to the "falsely" fanciful in a world where profundity either terrifies or seems to have long ago absconded?

HAPPY BIRTHDAY,
MICKEY MOUSE

by Ignatz Mouse

☐ OK, it galls me that I have to remind you that *I* was once famous, star of a comic strip that I gallantly allowed my second tomato, Krazy Kat, to headline. But, OK, feature this, and it will all replay for you: I threw a brick at Krazy's noggin. The *skillfully* aimed brick lands; the Kat thinks, *he loves me;* and our town's lawman, Offissa Pup, kat-smitten, tosses me in the hoosegow. *Fin.* What delirious variations we rang on those few chords! If I do say so myself. Which I have to, because we haven't appeared in Hearst papers since 1943.

So I, Ignatz Mouse, am locked away in this tiny Arizona town, untimely retired, the only mail in forty years a letter from a magazine, saying why don't I wish sixty-year-old Mickey Mouse a rodent-to-rodent Happy Birthday! While Mickey—with his squeaky voice (and why *have* a voice, for Christ's sake, if all you are going to say is "Well, I'll be doggoned!")—appears as corporate pitchman on a veritable Kmart full of franchised plastic.

OK. But let's be clear why, if I'm so smart, he's so rich. I wouldn't compromise my art. Mickey would.

'Cause Mickey doesn't mean art; he means business. Business designed Mickey: simple-to-draw circles so Disney Studios could churn out miles of film. Mickey, the no frills, sans hair, Model T Mouse—his only detailing two big buttons on his shorts. I'm no Clark Gable, but *he*'s undistinguished oblongs, simple pipestem legs, and oversize clogs, "to give him the look," Uncle Walt says, "of a kid wearing his father's shoes." With typical toady self-hatred, Mickey donned white gloves so his hands would look more human—as if to say, congratulations homo sapiens, you're the ne plus ultra of a species! But there, too, the cost cutters snipped and Mickey has only four digits—"one less finger to animate." Imagine, surrendering a finger to make the production line move faster!

OK. At least in the 1930s, in halfway honest roles like Steamboat Willie, this streamlined critter was the happy symbol of the Necessities of the Machine we yearned to obey—if only the depression-dead assembly lines would roll again! But now, logoized, razor-cut, blown-dry, corporate spokesman Miki Mouse shows a new face: He's Smiley the Button. "Hi! I'm the facsimile of kindly feelings, worn to remind others that someone once had kindly feelings!" Mickey isn't even cute anymore, he just stands for the memory of cute, corporate symbol of a corporation that used to produce cute entertainment. How does it entertain us now? By producing those corporate symbols of a corporation that used to produce entertainment!

Krazy's whiskers brush my shoulder, as she sneaks a peek at what I'm writing. "If Mr. Disney Studios wanted to play with *you*, Mr. Ignatz Mouse, you'd do lunch like shot off a shovel!"

"Would not."

"Would."

"Would not."

"I like movies," Krazy says. "So do you. Look, let's snuggle on the couch and watch some Mickey cartoons."

"OK. Sure," I say. "By way of research." Besides, I like to watch Mickey on my VCR. At the movie theater, you can't take your eyes off the screen, you'll miss something, so you can't think, the movie injects its thoughts right into your head, and even I start to smile at Mickey. But, once again, keepitallism sells us the tape to hang it with. Now I can stop Mickey. I can *think* about Mickey. I can even solarize him!

So here's Mickey, in *The Mail Pilot,* and *Clock Cleaners,* and running a tugboat, with his pals Goofy and Donald, and putting out a fire, and, frankly, this trio of innocence, anger, and stupidity can't do anything right. "Well, I'll be doggone," Mickey says as the clock explodes, the fire destroys everything, the boat sinks. These guys are no Stan and Ollie, they're not too silly, or too anarchic, or too instinctual for their jobs, they're just too inept. That's Mickey's appeal—no threat, useless but decorative, a bimbo's bimbo. The only one I *can* stomach is Donald, whose sqwaaks resonate with tangy disgust. But Donald's the spoonful of vinegar that helps the sugar go down. Duck meat makes the stew sweet and sour instead of sickly sweet and that just sells more stew.

Meanwhile Ms. Kat, black paw warmly encircling me, giggles. I would brick her if we could sell even one ticket for something as honest and troubling and ambiguous as that. But that's why *we*'re not in Hollywood, we created real, hot, *unsettling* feelings in our audience. "Look," Krazy says, "Mickey can hardly stand up in those big shoes," and like a fool I look at the T.V., where Minnie is "unintentionally" showing her bloomers, and think, well, gee, Mickey, don't fall now! You have to save Minnie from stubbly-faced Black Bart! . . . God, what's happening, I have to stick my nails into my paw, like Michael Caine in the *Ipcress File,* or I'm going to be kitschnotized by Mickey. Then Mickey will command me to smile at Mickey, to show the world I'm a nice kid-loving guy, the kind who smiles at Mickey (even though he's not that hilarious, even though I don't really feel like smiling), but it's too late, my hand is moving in the air as if I'm petting something, and before I can stop Krazy sees, and winks fondly at me, thinking I must be a nice guy. . . . Well, I am, if she thinks I am, aren't I? . . . Poor little Mickey, that was a funny bit, wasn't it, when the whole band was carried away by a tornado and crescendoed up into the sky? . . . This "Band Concert" is pretty good, I hope Mickey and Donald will be OK when they decrescendo down. . . . Be OK? What am I talking about! That mouse is worth kabillionjillion dollars! Wait, I know how to stop this, I'll pull those little two-button pants down, I'll show them I'm not nice, I'll rape him in, in the, in the . . . ear, or the nose, somewhere beyond perversion, something *awful,* but I don't even really *want* to do it, I'm just trying to fight this sweet lethargy that says, show people you're no sourpuss, give the hairless rodent a hug while Krazy takes a Polaroid for mom. . . . Show them I'm nice, show 'em I'm bad. Kitschy Mouse makes feelings into show-and-tell, and dries up the true well springs of desire. . . . But that's silly sourpuss talk, I guess, 'cause Krazy loves Mickey, everyone loves Mickey, 'cause he's so adorable in those little pants with their two buttons, I can't take my eyes off those two buttons, I just want to own something that has two-button pants, and, oh, gosh, it's Mickey's birthday, and, well I'll be doggone, I almost forget! I want to buy Mickey a card that's really cute, to show everyone I love him, something, say, with a picture of Mickey Mouse on it! a Mickey card for Mickey to say Happy Birthday, Mickey, you dear little bitty (wait, help me! I'm melting! I'm melting!) itty (whoa! dig those nails in, Ignatz, believe the pain! Pain, only pain, is ever the real you in this rotten world!) . . . pear-shaped (yah! that's better, that's the ticket, Ignatz!) . . . chicken-biting (OK, that feels right, more *Ignatian*) . . . gawk! . . . (gawk? wait, I mean gick! . . . no, wait, dig those nails in, Ignatz! you can do it, U be U!) . . . geek!

Whew, free at last!

"Darlink," Krazy says, taking my scarred paw in hers to kiss it better, and with a new glint in her eyes that I think *I* maybe sometimes gleamed with in my own brick throwing days, "got any more Mickey cartoons?"

EATING DISORDERS

☐ When I go to the movies my heart fills with intense expectation, and for the first half hour or so of almost any movie I am unreasonably pleased, so in awe of the wonderful technology of the spectacle, of a world so accurately reproduced yet enlarged, that I think I'm watching a great movie, when really I am just—at least for a while—delighted by the glamour of movies. I gawk at the sheer size and light of the thing, as if what was shown escaped mere representation, *as if* I were not seeing images but something like the delicious body of the world itself. (But better: no need to fear the anxiety caused by another body.)

I gawk at the stars' glamour, too, an aura the more mysterious to me because it comes not from their beauty (stars are often far from pretty), but from their magnificent self-absorption, an attitude so long perfected that it seems almost generous of them to show themselves to me. The star has learned to want herself first, learned to love the shape of her own nose, its cunning little bump; and I love her for seeming to love herself—a masochistic passion, for that very quality means she will never need or love me. So large, so smooth (the screen shows abrasions and crannies yet remains forever unbroken, like the most perfect skin), so whole (all on one plane, she and her world are a perfect fit), the star is inedible by me or by time. By comparison, I'm needy, cracked, vulnerable, hungry; and my shame at my body only adds to the star's glamour. (And how fans abused Elizabeth Taylor for betraying stardom by being hungry, getting fat!)

But a desire to see glamour is only a small part of my excited expectation at the movies; and perhaps, too, it's the empty food I accept when I know my more profound appetites won't be fed. For mostly my heart leaps to greet a film because I expect to be *transformed* by the meeting. At the movies, I expect (though it rarely happens) to find new fragments (of style, of attitude, of gesture, of magical fantasy) to add to the inner assemblage that *is* my psyche, fragments that properly assembled might be curative of those first images of union and of severance that have shaped me. For I like the psychoanalytic view of the self (maybe because it reminds me of movies), that the personality is a raggle-taggle montage of the unlikely fantasy-images and pieces of the world that, out of love and fear of loss, you swallowed up in childhood—a delicious breast, a moustache, a comforting fragment of a cloth coat you once felt against your cheek, a melodramatic threatening hand, a melancholy carriage to the body. Supposedly one often gets such fragments at films, so that after a movie, members of the audience leave the theater walking like James Dean, mumbling like Brando, but in my experience the images are too perfect, too hard to be truly broken up, mixed with the saliva of the imagination, and swallowed.

I know it's a fairy tale expectation to think that I'll find magical fragments to remake the mosaic of myself at my local mall's wickedly uncomfortable octoplex. And, of course, I'm almost always disappointed. After an hour, I twist about in my seat. We've been cheated! There's nothing transformative here, nothing nourishing! I turn back to the screen, and in the absence of food, I accept more glamour; but it tastes a little bitter to me.

Once upon a time, though, I think many people felt that popular culture gave them something more to feed upon, something to help them in their remaking. In the Sixties, it was as if Bob Dylan or the Beatles or Aretha Franklin were growing up before us, and sent back, as if from the front line of a new adulthood, reports of their discoveries and their quandaries. A *new adulthood,* or so we thought (and *not* just a Peter Pan–like endless childhood), with an insistence that morality and ecstasy could be reconciled, that the questions of pleasure (what are its sources? how is the deepest pleasure to be formed? how are we to be worthy of it? what are its dangers?), if sounded deeply enough, pursued rigorously enough, would instruct us in how to shape a new human solidarity. We even thought that the joys of art might lead us to a new rationality, a reason of the heart, where pleasure would guide the connections between realms, and satisfying organic form would be as rigorous in setting limits as any imposed order. In this enterprise, rock & roll drew heavily on—or stole from—black popular music, for nowhere else have the questions of pleasure been as profoundly asked as in black secular and gospel music, where to move together might make a congregation, and pleasure and morality join in the ecstasy of bodily possession by the holy spirit. Maybe that spirit can take one both in church and on the dance floor; in the Sixties black secular and religious combined to make "Soul" music, the most enthralling and wrenching popular art of that time.

There was oodles of *Teen Scene Magazine* illusion in our sense of connection with popular artists, but not just that—though the artists did grow rich (and distant) from our adoration. Still, the artists' wealth seemed less important to us than the questions we thought we shared, as if money merely gave them greater scope and leisure to carry out experiments on our behalf. And what they discovered, we were sure, would be—like sex, the three basic rock & roll chords, or a hit of windowpane acid—cheap thrills, democratically available. After all, why should beauty only be rare and difficult?

I also had a sense of questions shared, of bits of answers for us to use within our selves in the filmed essay-stories, the research reports, of Jean-Luc Godard, and in the more generous, more sweet-tempered films of the Yugoslav filmmaker Dujan Makavejev. And Makavejev remains especially valuable to me in his continuing attempt, through the greedy Eighties, to rally the scattered dispirited remnants of the party of pleasure. Even in his less successful films the questions remain: What is the instruction pleasure might offer? Why do we fear it? What is the shape of the community pleasure might make? And will it look grotesque to our eyes? (So much the worse for our eyes!)

Makavejev's greatest films are *WR: Mysteries of the Organism*, a free form fantasia-documentary inspired by Wilhelm Reich (patriarch—or sacred monster—of the party of pleasure), and *Sweet Movie*, an original mixture of allegory, fantasy, and documentary. These films of the early Seventies describe, in terms witty, shrewd, vulgar, and blatant, the ways we've tried to free our bodies, and the ways history has mutilated them. *Sweet Movie* follows a special "Miss World" pageant, whose winner's prize will be marriage to the richest man in the United States. (His pleasure is the degradation of his wife. To consummate the marriage he'll reward her with a urinous "golden shower.") Alongside this story we follow the ship of Captain Anna Planeta (CP), called *Survival,* as it moves forward through a city's canals with a hugh papier-mâché bust of Karl Marx on its prow. To lure people on board she promises them open-hearted comradeship, sensual plea-sure, redemption on this earth for their bodies. That is to say, the Communist Party coopts comrades from the party of plea-sure. This time she attracts a fellow named "Bakunin," from the ship *Potemkin,* representing the early, and betrayed, promise of the Russian revolution; and with sweets and a striptease she also seduces three teenage boys to join her. The party of pleasure, it seems, is ripe for betrayal; desperate to deny the death instinct, the attraction of the gun pointed at others or at oneself, it makes ecstasy too easy a matter, purg-ing it of all violence. So the repressed returns: "Bakunin" willingly submits to what he knows will be the deadly caresses of Captain Planeta. She bites his neck, and he says, "That's good, go on. . . . Everything cannot be explained . . . I felt so jealous when Vakovlinchuk was killed." Then she stabs him to death in a bath of sugar. "I brought a lot of sugar," CP complains later, "but I can't get rid of the bitter taste." She murders the teenagers and has the crew put a tear under Marx's eye.

We also join a commune in Amsterdam for a saturnalian meal of the greatest grotesqueness, a theatrical counterculture dinner whose intent feels therapeutic. At this feast a commu-nard takes a huge sausage out of his pants, lays it across the table, and whacks slices off for everyone with a big knife; communards drink urine, and vomit freely; a man shits on a platter, and his bowel movement is carried about as the "Ode to Joy" plays in the background. This carnival of a world and a body turned upside down is followed by a painfully literal and self-conscious ceremony of rebirth in which a fat, hairy man, covered with blood and feces, has his comrades beat on his stomach to mimic the painful contractions of giving birth—in this case, to himself. The whole community swaddles, powders, and nurses him as he mewls and pukes. (Rebirth is celebrated. But the other stages of life, the *deathward* ones, as we ripen and rot, seem once again omitted.) The communards then dance with a hippety-hop motion that filled me alternately with a desire to move with them, and a wish, like Miss World—who becomes anorexic at the commune—to get as far away as possible (perhaps to sell real estate and watch T.V.). At the conclusion of the film Captain Planeta is arrested, and the corpses arise again, like the countries of Eastern Europe. Is their rebirth only a trick of the camera? Are they alive, or not yet alive? That decision (and the how and why of rebirth) is left to the viewer.

Makavejev's next film, *Montenegro,* was released in 1981, as the once frolicsome party of pleasure—including delegates from the left misled by Anna Planeta, weary former communard feasters from the counterculture, gay erotic adventurers afraid of sexually transmitted diseases (and the growing rumor of worse to come)—became tuber audiences to a T.V.-provided history. (With T.V. you needn't fear the anxiety caused by another body.)

In *Montenegro,* Susan Anspach frighteningly incarnates an American housewife in Sweden, Marilyn Jordan, wife of Martin and mother of two, thoroughly uncomfortable in very comfortable circumstances. She runs away with a theatricalized theater troop of Yugoslav immigrants, has an affair with one of them—Montenegro—murders him, and returns home to poison her family.

"There is enough food in this country," a customs inspector says, confiscating a young immigrant girl's pig. Probably there is; but Makavejev wonders if it's good to eat. Near the beginning of the film, Anspach offers a bowl of milk laced with poison to the family dog. "It's your decision," she says to the dog. "But if you ask my advice don't do it." And her husband's grandfather, who has been made wacky by time and American pop culture until he thinks he's Buffalo Bill, looks suspiciously at the glass of milk that Marilyn brings him, and says, "What is in this milk?" (In fact, it's the grapes that they should all be looking out for, that's where she'll place the poison.) Would *we* know the right food? This film's flavor is not the unsatisfying bitterness of glamour, but an irony that tastes to me like spoiled milk, a sourness that comes, I think, from a distrust of the ecstasies that Makavejev and I had, we fear, once foolishly found nourishing, yet fear we might be more foolish to surrender. So we grow to doubt our ability to tell good food from bad, as if the rottenness were in us as well, in our judgment.

That a woman should offer poisoned food to her family is almost unbearable to me. There must be an explanation! Something must have curdled her milk. I first saw the film as a story—more or less—of a woman's failed liberation: an oppressive husband, a try at independence of a wife driven so mad that she was unable to bear the food (the delicious lamb, the strong, illegal brandy) of freedom. In this version of the film the emblematic dialogue is the obtuse businessman's telephone conversation with his runaway wife, whom he believes has been kidnapped: "Will they [the imagined kidnappers]

accept a check? How much do they want? It must be a fortune!" To which Marilyn angrily replies, "It's more than you
can begin to afford, my darling." (Martin doesn't mean to be
disparaging by counting Marilyn's cost; that his wife would be
worth a fortune to the imagined kidnappers also measures her
worth to him.)

Marilyn's madness made me anxious, and I wanted to calm
my nerves by *explaining* her. But my interpretation was too
bland, already chewed. And a contrary outcome to Marilyn's
failure, the many victories for independence won by the
women's movement, hadn't so far at least, led to the triumph
of pleasure. So I went back to the film wondering what made
Marilyn destroy her ecstasy and poison others.

I thought, too, this might tell me something about why the
party of pleasure has faded so. The explanation for Marilyn's
unhappiness would be one answer to Freud's question—by
now, I think, his most quoted phrase—which is also one of the
movie's questions: *what does woman want?* Perhaps the questions of pleasure can be phrased in this way because women's
pleasure has been found threatening for so long (by men—and
perhaps sometimes by women, too), and because our earliest
memories of pleasure are bound up with a woman's body.

This time I think that it's film (that often disappointing but
still crucial ecstasy), the means by which her story is told, that
has curdled Marilyn Jordan, made her murderous towards her
pleasure. (And it is, as I say, a drug I frequently consume, too!)
So the movie *intends* to leave a bad taste in my mouth, for the
film's not just about Marilyn Jordan poisoning others, but
about film poisoning me. Makavejev wants to warn me against
his own medium; perhaps he dreams, too, that film might be
the kind of poison that, used properly, might cure.

Each art, during the course of its development (and even—

as *Don Quixote* shows in the case of the novel—near its beginning, before a sense of its dangers was drowned by the din of its triumphs, its effective distractions), has offered warnings, and homeopathic cures for the diseases that the art itself might cause. *Madame Bovary* (whose irony is at least as unsettling in flavor as Makavejev's) is the nearly poisonous narrative that would be the cure for romantic narratives. Brecht wished to make theater an instrument against the distractions—the harmful identifications and soporific inattention to one's actual bitter conditions—that theater produced. Godard's films borrow Brecht's techniques, and his characters, self-consciously the children of Marx and Coca-Cola—which is to say, of film—reproduce for us the "automatisms" caused by a love affair with the mechanical medium, movies. Each of these artists sometimes directly, in exposition, in plot, or in allegories that describe the medium of the story even as the story is told, warn us of the dangers of artistic representation, and produce from this doubled message about their own medium an anxious quality and a sense of depth. It's a difficult job *to film* the dangers of film, and not simply to theatricalize one's self-suspicion—making the critique of the show another part of show business. (I think something like that happens, for example, in Antonioni's *Blow-Up.*) But most recent movies—like the Eighties retro-style Hollywood films—don't try to critique their medium. They seem simply nostalgic for earlier representations, and just want to repeat them to manufacture a flat distraction in the present. (But in this endless Peter Pan–like second childhood you'll have money to buy better toys, niftier special effects.)

In *Montenegro* film becomes the subject near the beginning of the story, in Marilyn Jordan's kitchen, as she cooks dinner for her family. Marilyn furiously pounds veal as if all the hatred of her life could be put into the mallet's swing, and then, in one of the more chilling scenes in a very frosty film, she teaches her daughter a recipe, as if she was teaching the little girl a witch's curse. But, as in a fairy tale, the witch's curse imprisons the witch: "This life," Marilyn concludes angrily, "this movie—all so damn predictable." The child asks, "What movie?" Marilyn replies, "The movie we're in." The child demurs, "I'm not in a movie. I'm in the kitchen." And Marilyn concludes, frighteningly, "In the kitchen like the schnitzel in the hot fat." Then we see Marilyn eating a pile of schnitzel, eating, as we find out later, *all* of her family's dinner, and as she tears at the meat she looks both dazed and imprisoned, an empty spirit in vacant space.

Makavejev is always fascinated by how we animals eat. In the communal meal in *Sweet Movie* the communards grossly, savagely, conflate eating and defecation and sex. Which is which, and where? Where does it come from, and where does it go, and what farcical torments must we go through if we are ever to get it right? In *Montenegro* there's a small reprise of the commune's feast when we watch the Jordans stuff themselves with spaghetti till it tumbles out of their mouths, while the young son gleefully describes a Frenchman who died gorging himself on snails. The Jordans seem to be having a good time, but they would be shocked if they saw how grotesque they looked. (The communards of *Sweet Movie* would be shocked, I think, if they *hadn't* looked grotesque to me.)

I'm not sure that the director has some settled position on how or what we should eat, except that he doesn't want to let us forget that we are animals when we eat (as, of course, we always are). Starting from our animality might be a way to discover a deeper, though for the moment uncomfortable, sense of solidarity, and even, perhaps, possibilities for more satisfying activity. So food provides Makavejev with many ways to phrase the questions of pleasure: What are good table manners (that is: a decent—sometimes *too* decent—social order) and what is our proper food? (Why do we feel hungry all the time, our bodies unsatisfied?) Eating is a metaphor, too, for how we symbolically feed upon the body of the world to form ourselves, swallowing bits we like to form the montage of the self. (Why can't we find better pieces to add to our montage?) So eating is the infant's first version of the question of how pleasure might make the self, and Makavejev continues, often in an infantile way, the child's investigations: *Do I feed upon her destructively?* becomes, must we waste each other, in work and in sex? Or, to give a utopian extension to his metaphor, is there some way that the dream of the communion meal might become real on this earth, so that the communards might joyously eat and joyously offer themselves, through all that their bodies can do, as symbolic food?

Marilyn—we learn as we watch her devour the family's schnitzel—is voracious. And she thinks herself imprisoned; not by her husband, precisely, but because she's in a movie, trapped there—as if she were food—like schnitzel in hot fat. Of course, she *is* in a movie, one directed by Dujan Makavejev; made up of images, she is an image, and what she eats is an image. No wonder her appetite is so unappeasable—is there an image *of* food that can satisfy? A woman who is "in a movie," a woman made up of images, is a version of the person (common outside movies, too) who acts "as if" she feels; so her emotions are only what she successfully portrays for others, what they take her as portraying. Severed from the inner sources of her own appetites, she can never be satisfied or truly satisfy.

This schnitzel scene reminded me of the gluttons' punishment in Dante's hell; they fall all over themselves in their rage to stuff mud in their mouths. Of course the "food" doesn't satisfy them, so they have to eat more and more of it. After Freud, though, I think Dante's sinners might, like the rest of us, be analyzed more remissively. The punishments that Dante doles out are not the result of their crimes, but their cause. They were voracious here on earth because the food they were given was like mud to them, and couldn't satisfy. Neither the glutton nor an anorexic like "Miss World" can find the food they truly want to eat. (And perhaps they sometimes poison others, so they, too, won't be satisfied.)

When I was watching Anspach's angry, bewildered face, I wondered why Makavejev had made his damned glutton an American. (Of course, I mean *Marilyn's* face, but when a movie performance so seems to fit the actor's body I forget which is role and which the player. Bogart becomes Hammett becomes Sam Spade. John Wayne becomes the American West embodied, a hero off screen because he walked like a hero on screen.) Is Makavejev unfairly having at us, as if we Americans poisoned others because we were too puritanical, or too prudent, and couldn't stand our own pleasure? Miss World, for example, Makavejev's representative American lass in *Sweet Movie*, can't fuck for business reasons; her "cherry" is, she feels, her most saleable asset. But what country revels more—however restlessly—in its hedonism? Have we really created bodies so made for work, or so intolerant of the flesh, that we're incapable of pleasure? I think we have to grant Makavejev that we *are* restless, yearning, dissatisfied, and perhaps (more than some puritan stain) it's because we've given ourselves over to the endless teasing of the spectacle, to images *as* commodities, and commodities as mostly images— so a thing is as much the brand name, and the fantasy of its advertising, as it is the work it might do. The ability to anneal trademark and product is part of the genius of images—like film's ability to unify the character and the actor. "When people eat chocolate, the brand we advertise . . . I want them to feel they're eating you," one mock movie director in *Sweet Movie* says to Miss World, as she's filmed circling her breasts with chocolate. But when you buy the product, you don't really get the delicious body of the world itself, you're *not* really eating it. This sort of symbol—product + image—can be bought, but not eaten, for this symbol wasn't meant to be used *by* you in your self-construction. (It was meant to shame you.)

This describes, in part, the inevitable dissatisfaction of human sexuality, which, like advertising, begins in fantasy. We dream of the breast when it isn't there; when it returns the real isn't *quite* the same as our star-fantasy, not as perfectly satisfying as what we had imagined. So image-culture's airbrushed fantasies play upon the disappointment of sexuality, magnify it, intensify it to the point of a restless insatiable madness. The images, compared to *our* bodies, rebuke us for our gross appetites (we're so imperfect, so needy compared to the stars). And the images, compared to the food we might find, seem so perfect, so flawless, yet, when we try to use them they are, because of that very perfection, so inedible, so unsatisfying!

Perhaps if you bought *enough* image-commodities they might, almost, turn your own body into something watched— so although you can't *use* the images within yourself, you might almost *become* one. Swaddled in designer clothes you can have, for a few moments, the feeling that you're in an ad, have become a hard enduring image, an immortal self-satisfied movie star, rid of the muck and appetites of the body, neither eating nor being eaten. (Or, like Marilyn, you might feel you're trapped in a movie.) As Alex, the Yugoslav pater-familias, says to Marilyn—when she has, by a nice concatenation of plotting, gone to live with the immigrants at their theater-compound, "Many people have Gucci shoes. You have a Gucci foot." He means this as a compliment, but it's also another curse, for not just the shoe you wear, he is saying, but the foot itself, has become a brand name, an image in a spectacle—a star's foot, masochistically loved by Alex because it doesn't need him; it requires no tickling, no fondling.

Marilyn's husband, worried by his wife's endless dissatisfaction, seeks out a psychiatrist for her, Dr. Aram Pazardjian. This doctor, with his bowl-cut white hair and enigmatic smile, is a creepy charismatic fraud who looks remarkably like Andy Warhol. Dr. Pazardjian's power (and perhaps some of Warhol's as well) comes from an open admission of fraudulence. "He would like you to know," his receptionist says, demanding payment in advance, "that he is only interested in money." In this free display of his vulgarity he is like the Yugoslavs Marilyn will meet later; after long denial, such open vulgar appetite, such bad taste, can be a new and fascinating flavor. (O my Madonna, my newfound land!)

Dr. Pazardjian feeds Marilyn a few gnomic fortune cookies —"what's the difference between one chicken?" and "How long is a piece of string?" Marilyn's need to be joined to a saving power turns Dr. Pazardjian into a healer who cares about her, so she tries to answer his K mart koans. To the first she replies, "You mean a chicken looking in a mirror?" Then "You can't escape someone if that someone happens to be yourself." And in reply to the second, she mimes hanging herself.

She is saved from more therapy when, accidentally stranded

at an airport, she's serendipitously taken up by the Yugoslav immigrants who I think of as Gypsies—for in tales of a housewife who needs to be saved from her husband it is often the Gypsies who fulfill the role. The Yugoslavs are, as it turns out, a charming troop of performers. Part of their sweetness is a gift of the moviemaker: The bourgeois household has been shot in very harsh light, and fill-light has been used throughout to give a cold, evenly lit, inedible, almost clinical effect to the scenes. The immigrants, by contrast, are shot in smoky, soft, romantic light. And like the commune in *Sweet Movie,* the immigrants' encampment-showplace (ZanziBar) is a libidinous soup. The *Sweet Movie* communards' attempt to recapture, to reawaken their bodies (are we alive or dead?) was frightening, grotesque, willful, and repulsive in their purgative, shitting, puking effort to get all the bad stuff out of themselves. This group of Slav performers seems to have been given a pass on history; easy in their appetites, they have nothing to mend. By contrast to *Sweet Movie*'s cock-sausage, the lamb that we've seen Montenegro carry across his back, butcher, roast, and serve at ZanziBar simply looks delicious. (In the Makavejev film that follows this, *The Coca-Cola Kid,* the drama of an American placed among the libidinal denizens of a forest of Arden is played out, even more improbably, by contrasting a tightly wound American businessman— brilliantly played by Eric Roberts—with . . . Australians. Makavejev, I think, has grown desperate for "a world elsewhere"—anywhere! In this Makavejev reminds me of the way radicals turned about looking for allies and noble saviors free of society's distortions—schizophrenics? women? blacks? students? the third world? . . . Australians?)

In ZanziBar Gypsies brawl with elemental anger, take knives in the head and blows from a shovel across the skull—

but no one dies. And sexual play, in its free unfolding, causes no anxiety: Alex and a woman fuck athletically at the bottom of the bed where Marilyn sleeps; the bed collapses, enraging the young woman, who then snuggles under the covers with Marilyn. ("What do we need him for?" the woman says of Alex, as she pets Marilyn. "That feels good," Marilyn replies with a quizzical but accepting look.) ZanziBar is rich in moments of charming communal improvisation. At the airport Marilyn has broken a heel from her shoe, so Alex's former wife slips hers off to provide for the guest. If Marilyn needs a towel for the shower, the ex-wife whisks a tablecloth into service.

The slippers that Alex's ex-wife gives Marilyn fit; this Cinderella story ends darkly, but it's filled with fairy tale elements. At the airport, for example, Martin doesn't recognize his wife's broken shoe, even when it is held in front of his face by Alex: this certifies Martin's unsuitability. At ZanziBar, after a battle over her, Marilyn revives a seemingly dead Montenegro, thus showing they're fated for each other.

Makavejev has always liked the style of fairy tales. *Sweet Movie,* for example, retells "Hansel and Gretel": the bad witches of both capitalism and communism use and distort our desire for sweets to lure us to our destruction. Communism promises the "real" sweetness of a satisfying community, then pushes its citizens into the gulag. Capitalism coats its images with a patina of sex to make its products seem sweet, but the world then becomes images that can't satisfy. I think Makavejev is drawn to fairy tales because in them the characters' (and the reader's) unconscious wishes suddenly, surprisingly become symbols, fragments of fantasy rich with one's unknown necessities for connection and for death, magical food and drink that can change one's personality. . . . Or does

Marilyn simply delude herself about her suitability for Montenegro—as one might say sarcastically, "She's trying to turn life into a fairy tale"? Are such stories of ecstatic transformation (like my memories of Sixties popular culture) just self-deception? Makavejev's irony, which tastes to me like my own self-distrust, makes it hard to decide.

Maybe Makavejev simply loves his theatrical Gypsies because they're a better subject for the camera than the world outside ZanziBar. He has always had a goat's appetite for popular stagecraft, bawdy songs, vulgar burlesque. And unlike their intuitive sexuality, the Slavs weren't simply born more colorful, for Makavejev shows us how they have *made* themselves interesting—whatever the risks—as part of their seductive vaudeville. A photo they take of themselves, for example, before rushing a wounded man to the hospital makes a more engaging snapshot than the Kodak of the family Marilyn has left, because in the Gypsies' Polaroid one of the characters has a knife sticking out of his head. They're willing to die for their picture, for only the knife in the head allows the Gypsies to compete with the many other entertainments available to us. (But in ZanziBar, if it weren't for the beautiful American, no one need really *die.*)

Is it only me (and not the director) who's suspicious of Makavejev's recent worlds elsewhere, his ZanziBar, his "Australia" (still green because the Americans, the Coca-Cola Corporation, haven't eliminated the charming native softdrinks)? These Gypsies remind me sometimes of a fond memory of communal living, which, in reality, did give many ecstatic moments but also had more of the actual slog and abrasion of people living together than ZanziBar does. (Why are there never any towels not spotted with Chianti, or any dry tablecloths!) And sometimes, in their efforts to theatricalize themselves, the Slavs remind me, too, of the way so many in the Sixties seemed greedy for publicity, made themselves grotesque in order to become good subjects for the camera. The party of pleasure's desire to purge ecstasy of its destructiveness, its wish to deny the death instinct, contributed greatly to this lust to become an image—for images, like stars, need never die.

These desperate performers stay alive by entertaining people—as Martin does with the mass-produced "sculptures" he sells ("ball bearings in a straitjacket," the psychiatrist calls them), as Dr. Pazardjian does with his gnomic patter, as the pathetic applicants to be Buffalo Bill's wife do when they mug for the video camera that Martin's children hold on them. All the world's a stage. In *The Coca-Cola Kid,* the Coca-Cola executive wants an "authentic Australian sound" for his T.V. ads, and on the street in Sydney he finds a fairy tale character, a raggedy gray-bearded aboriginal gnome who plays a horn made at the beginning of time. Of course, the musician offers the executive his business card, and asks him to get in touch with his agent.

Probably, like me and the aborigine, the Gypsies have agents, too, for they're greedy for things as well as for attention. Several of the women want Marilyn's fur coat, the young girl wants her hair done to look like Marilyn's, and Alex wants to sleep with her because "she's a lady." But these simple greeds are easy enough to accept. It isn't so much that our greeds ensnare us (though they do, they did!), or that, as Lenin wrote, the small bourgeois ceaselessly gives rise to the large, but that the small theater troop goes to Broadway, the Polaroid picture dreams of becoming the De Mille epic, and the ZanziBar vaudeville show probably wants to use our adoration to grow rich and distant from us and become part of what

makes us at once yearning, passive, and dissatisfied, become
. . . television. As, alas (whether Makavejev wants it or not),
did *Montenegro*. The last time I saw the movie, it was on cable
T.V.'s Movie Channel—introduced by an "as if" good-old-
boy, Joe Bob Briggs, on his "Drive in Theater Show." "Joe
Bob" had once been a Texas newspaperman who reviewed
grade C movies in a comic red-neck persona. But the man and
the mask annealed, and the reporter was fired when Joe Bob's
reviews grew offensively racist and misogynist. (Some men
wear fancy boots, but Joe Bob had grown shit-kicker feet.)
He's made a comeback on cable. Last week, Joe Bob announced, the programmers had goofed and sent him a foreign
film. Still, it wasn't as bad as he thought it would be. It had,
he said, eight shots of naked breasts.

The second act of the Gypsy show includes several of the
naked breasts as a young girl does a striptease, clearly enjoying
her own performance. There isn't any innocence to be found
in Makavejev's movies. He thinks that's another fantasy, like
table manners, or movie stars, that people use to repress themselves, for they fear their pleasure. (Such magical eating might
change us, and we want to remain forever as we are, never
dying.) The young girl is chased by a plastic penis on wheels
until she submits to being mock-fucked by it, and is fork-lifted
into the heavens above the stage. Marilyn is then carried off
by her prince charming, her legs wrapped around him in the
most shamelessly clichéd pose of romantic pornography, like
the trashy novel we'd seen her reading in bed with her husband. The smoky light and tinkley music of this shot may
mark that the director knows this is hokum, Marilyn's cliché-
fantasy of satisfaction. But is it Makavejev's, too? And if *I* still
find it hokey is it because I fear pleasure now? Or because I
snobbishly disdain honky-tonk thrills, the grade C movies that

I, too, once had a goat's appetite for—just because they want to be on television? (And where do I want to be?)

Marilyn, angry at her own need, produces a scene for her internal theater where she has protested her desire, where she has no appetites, where she was—in the scenarios she's staging for her super-ego—taken against her will. She hits Montenegro in the most theatrical of ways. Then they fuck, rolling about in the grain. Fireworks—literally!—go off outside their bedroom, the climax to the Gypsy show. Again, like the tinkley music, this is an irony, undercutting the glorious "did the earth move?" aspect of their fucking—yet, like so much irony, allowing us also to *have* the sweet romantic feeling without thinking ourselves simpletons. After more fireworks—*feu d'artifice*—the show ends. The next morning, Marilyn walks out of ZanziBar, and we see Montenegro's body, his blood pouring out on the ground. Was Marilyn angered because she was satisfied with him—so she *has* needs (she isn't a star)? Or because he didn't please her—for how could an image satisfy? Is she terrified by her ecstasies (she isn't an image, she will die) or maddened by their absence (she remains trapped in a movie, surrounded by unsatisfying images)? Enraged, she's taken a knife to the screen, but now that we are ourselves a scene seen, she's also ripped into flesh.

In a talk of Makavejev's on Ingmar Bergman he said: "From Tausk's 1919 paper 'On the Origin of the Influencing Machine' we learn that each schizophrenic has his own all-powerful dictating machine. This machine is our genitals, projected and seen as foreign, determining our lives, the source of life. Bergman's depiction of the parts of a projector is his declaration of his machine, so conceived." The projector is the source of life—if life is an image. But if life is just an image—or *the wrong sort of image*—we can't incorporate it, but only watch it, and sink into a stupor of acceptance (of shame, and a yearning for glamour) and we grow ravenous. Or murderous.

Marilyn rejoins her family, and all she has done becomes a story around the dinner table. "There was a lamb that was slaughtered. . . . Two men fought a duel . . . she saved one of the men who was her lover."

Her son asks, does the story have a happy ending?

"Yes, they all lived happily ever after," Marilyn says, as is appropriate to a fairy tale become Hollywood movie.

But, a title tells us, the fruit she gives her family was poisoned—the grapes she gave her family, the apple Eve took, the movie we have watched.

Well, it's only a movie—in this case one in part about the dangers of movies. But then another title tells us that it's not just a movie. It was based on real events.

A troublesome ending; once again it left a bad taste, and not, this time, because of Marilyn's smiling savagery as she places poisoned grapes in her children's mouths. Once upon a time, I don't think Makavejev would have appealed to any authority outside of his fiction, wouldn't have thought that fiction was made *more* powerful, believable, by appealing to reality. Isn't it images used in some new way, images made more edible, made into symbols rich with our nutritive necessities, that may save us? I would think a filmmaker must believe so. Fantastic images (of castration, say) produced by our own Imaginary Film Company made us, and not *acceptance* of reality, but new fantastic images will remake us. We do have unconscious needs, of course, and only those fragments of fantasy will change us that embody those necessities; but I think Freud has shown us—and against his own wish for mastery—that there is no way, outside of fantasy, of metaphor and symbol, outside of finding the fairy tale elements in life, that those needs *can* be embodied (then eaten, incorporated) and our bodies re-formed. Do we feel we can no longer tell— let alone create!—a transformative fantasy from a glamorous momentarily pacifying, but eventually maddening, image?

There is in Makavejev's earlier films, like *Sweet Movie* and *WR: Mysteries of the Organism,* a conjunction, an intercutting of images of communism and of capitalism. Each revealed the failed attempt at re-formation within the other. But there *was* a failure each system suffered, and it was in its attempts at making the truth of utopia real on this earth, that is to say of making a world where our fantasies might be used by us to make ourselves, and not simply be sold to us in seemingly sweet but inedible images. Now I feel in my life, in Makavejev's recent movies, the lack of that revealing conjunction, the lack even of failure.

I count on Makavejev to find a way to ask the questions of pleasure again, and not give way, as he almost did in his next film, *The Coca-Cola Kid,* to despair. At the end of that movie, Eric Roberts is shocked from his faith in Coca-Cola (a product that has annealed for him with "the miracle of America . . . the American way of life") when a small Australian entrepreneur who made fine fizzy fruit drinks blows up his bottling plant and himself rather than have his factory taken over by Coke. Roberts quits the business world to set up house with the libidinally free daughter of the dead bottler, and her open-hearted child. They make a charming family unit. We see a mouse nose about a dollhouse, looking for a home. But the pleasures of home are, Makavejev thinks, less than we require. There is a world still to be changed by pleasure, till it satisfies our bodies. Or apparently Makavejev thinks we will destroy it: A title says, "A week later . . . while cherries blossomed in Japan/The next world war began." It *hasn't,* and most of the time I'm happy enough in my mouse house with my VCR and big-screen T.V. Occasionally, though, like a name I can't quite remember, I'm troubled by the fading specter of the party of pleasure's questions. (What was it they wanted to know about? food? . . . drink? . . . bread? . . . wine?) But I find it hard to imagine how one might now even ask such questions without sounding preposterous!

BLOOD

FOR THE

GHOSTS

☐   I began my novel *The Death of Che Guevara* after seeing some pictures in newspapers, and, in *Ramparts Magazine,* pictures of a guerrilla holding a child; of a guerrilla sitting with a peasant family on the ground outside a thatched roof hut; of a line of guerrillas disappearing into the long leaves of the jungle, the figures out of focus, blurred by motion. (The guerrillas loved to take photos; several rolls of undeveloped pictures were found in the dead men's knapsacks. Perhaps the film was a reassuring promissory note they offered themselves: *Someday*—still alive, far from here—we'll have these pictures printed. Perhaps, too, they enjoyed in advance the prospect of looking at themselves in fixed poses, an understandable plea-sure for people so endangered; the imagined snapshot viewer has survived the moment photographed.) I remember I looked hardest at the pictures taken by Guevara's captors, photos of Che's corpse inside a quonset hut, his chest exposed, a Bolivian general looking down on the corpse and holding a handkerchief to his nose; and of Che's corpse on a board, lying

across sawhorses, outside a laundry shed, in (I know) Valle-
grande, Bolivia, November, 1967. Now he is on display always,
in the photograph, to reassure the world that he is forever
there, in what suddenly feels to me like the placeless, eternal
past of the photograph. And we, looking at him, are now and
always still alive.

When I began writing about Guevara, around 1968, I was
not very aware of politics. Many friends, by contrast, had
thought and worked hard to end the war in Vietnam. Though
their understandings would have varied, they would have encompassed these pictures of Guevara in political terms. I was
moved more by the loneliness I imagined in the line of the
guerrillas disappearing into the jungle, just as I was moved,
when I read Che's journal, by his isolation, and his clarity as
he confronted his inevitable death. (The silent response of the
peasants to Che was, for him and the guerrilla movement he
led, like the symptom of a fatal disease.) Most of all, I was
transfixed by the image of his corpse, emaciated, holes in his
chest; his thin face wearing the vulpine look of the hungry
dead.

I think that most people's relationship to the history of our
time, its mass events and public figures, its marvels and its
horrors, comes, as mine did, through such images—newspaper photos, movies, T.V. news. Sometimes I think that this
continual consumption of images may make us feel immortal;
we can't really die because we're just watching; death is always
somewhere else. The often-remarked-on "weightless quality"
of contemporary experience results, I think, from this absence
of felt death in a world experienced as images. No death in the
image as one's own outward directed shaping violence (at
most one *shot* a camera). No death as one's own passing away
(the image, of whatever danger, remains outside oneself, in a

nowhere world as close as the screen, and as far away). No death as the final, irreparable passing away of the world (just rewind). So history happens right in front of us, and yet nowhere; rich in incident, yet no incident matters much; replete with tragic deaths, yet as if one never really dies.

So I was, in part (for there were certainly other motives that I won't write about here), drawn to the image of Che's corpse for the *nourishment* I ghoulishly thought it might offer me. In this essay I want to reflect on just that one aspect of my novel, that one ghoulish appetite—not on radical politics or the many different minds of Latin America, or the moral contest between violence and non-violence, or even the many particular contradictions that impelled Che Guevara, all of which are important to the novel. Here I want to think about—in the different and necessarily partial terms this essay must use— the way that my novel turns the theme of death this way and that, looking for what gifts that darkness might give.

To receive those gifts I would have to make Che's death substantial, felt, for myself and others, not—as the generals wished—as if he were forever dead, but as if his catastrophe were also mine. I had the partly borrowed intuition that to possess one's life one must live, as best one could, with the knowledge of its passing away. (Something grasped, usually, through a double—perhaps because otherwise the anxiety was unbearable.) This idea (though "idea" gives the feeling too much precision) came to me from the sorrowful lessons my own body had sometimes offered to teach me; perhaps it had come, too, not so much from fragments of Rilke and Heidegger, as from Hemingway; perhaps, also, I had that not uncommon adolescent idea that the war in Vietnam itself had lessons that I was debarred from (though that also marked my good fortune). Che had seemed to me someone who had lived with knowledge of his dying, so he was a pattern for that self-possession; and that knowledge seemed to give him what actors in the public realm usually lack, a sensibility. The corpse, one might say, had glamour, certainty, charisma because he had lived in relation to his death. He had had the good fortune to embody his questions very profoundly, and I think they were also profound questions, shaped by the *unresolvable* contradictions that make up the very texture of the self and the world. So his death *belonged* to him, an appropriate end to his life, and was with him, always, in the nature of the bloody experiment he had lived.

I wanted to reanimate the resistant image of Che, making it die again, and myself—symbolically!—with it, and so have a different, more intimate relationship to Che's death, as if that relationship might teach me a new relationship with myself. And with history—for to be in some small way part of a death (and a life) that mattered to so many would be a simulacrum of communion, I thought, with the forces that made history, what we sang of, in those euphoric and terrified times, as the "power of the people." (This dream of communion was also the dream of writing a book that would matter to many—a dream of a large audience!)

But a demon critic haunted my hand as I wrote. One shouldn't, he said, paste famous people into one's work, like colorized photos on a black and white page. Using historical figures in your novel, he said, meant that you couldn't make up a sufficiently interesting character on your own—and the creation of a character's sensibility is the glory of fiction. Instead, I was counting on the reader's interest in history, that already twice told tale, to generate interest in my story telling.

I think the demon critic is in some ways wrong. If we cannot enter imaginatively into history then it will become an intolerable burden to us—for before one can act, one must imagine that the world *might* be one's work. In a world overstuffed with images—with ourselves as outside the screen, as passive spectators—we begin to overcome our hypnotic fixation even by silk-screening a movie star's face, or doodling a moustache on a photo of the *Mona Lisa*. Or, perhaps, by making up a story about the picture of Che's corpse.

Still, the words of the demon critic stung; he spoke, I felt, from the heart of the novel genre. By which I mean—all perspectives in this matter being kept—I don't think one would mock Shakespeare because Richard the Third had a decided existence before he wrote. We're not even usually too hard on him for playing fast and loose with historical documents. Of course, this is because of the pleasure Shakespeare gives us—pleasures of language, of vivid villainy, of insight, of embodied ecstasies of selfhood. Shakespeare had, besides his genius, another advantage: when he wrote his history plays there was a nice fit between the form his time enjoyed, and one of the fundamental metaphors that shaped how one experienced public life and its actors. A time, that is to say, when all the world was a stage, and kings strutted the boards. (Was *his* world a spectacle, too? Perhaps, but not precisely in our sense; for, unlike film, one shares a space with the actors in a theater; one might, almost, mount the stage. And one might perform the play again, but not simply rewind it. Many people's cooperation would be necessary; the play would not be the same.)

Now, I think, the public world seems more like a machine. The public realm as a stage has been replaced by the heedless mechanism of the mass state. When the world began to seem like a machine, a new genre, the novel, came to entertain and instruct, to help us form our characters. Sensibility, which exists mostly at the cost of renouncing the savage intricacy of the machine-world, is, for the novel, a more important commodity than the worldly action that had filled Shakespeare's stage. The aristocratic ideal had been of power itself both creating and being created by "honor," an inwardness which implied a public register. It would be hard for me to name equivalents, for example, of Shakespeare's Henry the Fifth, or Richard the Second. True, Richard gains in sensibility as he discovers the hollowness of the crown, the public world. Yet I don't think in our time even a politician cast out of power could be granted—were the genius available—so much musing poetry.

In our increasingly diabolical world we can only suffer the machinery of the state, not operate it, but we can, at our best, be, like Christ, knowing, feelingful victims. In a footnote in a work of Arendt's—the volume *Imperialism* in her *Origins of Totalitarianism*—she writes: "[T]he drama became meaningless in a world without action. . . . Only the novel . . . developed all the gifts of modern sensitivity—for suffering, for understanding, for playing a prescribed role—which are so desperately needed by human dignity, which demands of a man that he at least be a willing victim if nothing else."

In the drama one needs other characters, to cue and to provide the context. One needs sets and setting. In the novel sensibility seems a personal possession—secretly shared by the writer, the character, and the reader. This inner life is expected to have little effect on public life. That is to say (as Beckett might) that the inner life has small public expression except for its own thwarting, its failure to express. Of course, one strand of this tale began long ago. Perhaps there was a world, Martin Buber writes in *Two Types of Faith,* where the soul was not yet a problem. The Law, and the community it founded, preceded the individual and named him. But the inwardness that was created by Paul and by Augustine makes faith the issue, and a soul is formed that others cannot know (for the world is a fallen one that has little place for one's soul) except by the declaration of faith which saves one—the assertion, whenever made, even at the last moment, that one believes. (Observance of the Law, from moment to moment, may justify one; the catechism saves one.) The community organized by moment-to-moment obedience to the community's Law ended for Christianity, and the world of faith—a faith that was a private possession, an inward matter primarily— began. What one does in order to have it seen by others—in prayer or in giving charity—is of no value. It is in how one declares one's faith in the story of Christ's willing suffering, his forsaking of the world in death, that the Christian is made. By belief in that death and that resurrection, we might gain eternal life. But what does "life" mean here? The screw tightens, and Luther asserts (or reasserts) that this world belongs to the devil, that salvation comes not by works ever, but by this relation only, by faith. Because the public world is renounced, or we've been sundered from it, sensibility—the innermost, the hidden, the true self—is forever an inward matter. But the only words are shared words, the words given usefulness by our form of life; lacking a shared, worldly dimension, the self may become ineffable. If one attempts to take hold of it, the true self flees, leaving traces only. (Innermost; hidden . . . but where?)

Novels create and display what public men surrender or never had—sensibility. The history of powerful, public persons is what the novel excludes—for history is no longer the action of individuals; history is what true individuals *suffer*. The novel disdains the public realm, with a bitter, ironic, proud, and resentful smile on its lips—the expression that Dostoyevsky's Underground Man might wear—as if to say, if I am to be excluded from action, then those who do act, or think they do, will be shown not only as producing consequences they did not intend and as the victims of those consequences, but as hollow men, without sensibility, without feeling.

Novels most often display the triumph for sensibility that, as Arendt says, is seized from worldly defeat by our being feelingful victims, *playing* our part in the machine, but knowingly, ironically. This plot is perhaps most poignantly realized in *Middlemarch,* through Dorothea, a character who can still imagine a public realm irrigated by sensibility, by compassion, but who is doubly excluded from a world that would, in any case, no longer resonate to a human sound. But it's more often the case that sensibility alone, with the barest memory of any other desire, is what the novel stages, the melancholy apprehension of the inevitable passage of time on which we will leave no mark. The gloomy characters of so much contemporary fiction would be hard pressed, I think, to say in what sort of world they might not endlessly suffer defeat, not because their demands are so ecstatic, but because the self has become altogether a song of loss; its substance is no more than the style of its defeat.

A novel about actors in the public realm begins to sound like an oxymoron. Yet some have achieved it. Perhaps the most brilliant resolution of this problem is Tolstoy's, who produced a historical character who acts, and who yet is not hollow, not unsympathetic. But General Kutúzov acts most effectively by not acting; he defeats Napoleon by himself endlessly retreating, by—like a hero of sensibility—burning his own cities, being, like Christ, a willing victim, immolating himself, and then (such is Tolstoy's genius) rising from those ashes, and becoming, by those ashes, victorious. Like Christ, he succeeds by failing. As for Che, his chest exposed, the ribs nearly poking through the skin—death made Che, that hard man, the political actor *as sufferer*. (He was not simply so, of course. Before he died he reportedly said to his executioner, "You are killing a man." And the Bolivian officer replied, "You have killed many men." Could I have allowed myself my attraction to him, if his actions hadn't ended in his death? Could I have accepted Che if he had been victorious, or would he have been revealed, then, as a characterless part of the state's machinery?)

It's difficult for me to think of many modern solutions to the problem of grafting the two uncrossable genres, the history of the powerful historical character, and the novel as the dark book of sensibility, difficult to think of many historical characters who are not hollow. If anything the emptiness has become more booming—the Stalin of *The First Circle* is far more buffoonish than Tolstoy's Napoleon. But there is for me in Solzhenitsyn's *Lenin in Zurich* such an ecstasy of hatred that the intensity of disdain provides a kind of sensibility for Lenin, a music heard in the hum of the diabolic machine.

For the most part, though, the powerful historical actor becomes the toy of the despised action genres, where he trails his glamour, and is not required to have a sensibility. When I think of these books I am reminded of Jean-Luc Godard's movie *1 + 1* (a film that warns us about film), where a tough guy voice narrates an endless pornographic, sadistic story, a comic-book political "thriller" where Brezhnev has sex with Kennedy, who is holding Marilyn Monroe hostage, who has a secret message for the Pope, who knows that Castro's mistress has slept with . . . etc., etc. The point being (I think) that politics is a soap opera plot of empty celebrity names, characters without insides. History is something like "Dallas" or "Dynasty" but spicier because there are "real" bodies involved. In works by William Buckley, or Douglas Terman—two such novels that I read because Che was a character of theirs as well—the problem of the historical *novelist* can just be surrendered; history needn't intersect with character, the pleasures of action are sufficient, and no one need have those combinations of thinking and feeling, of self-understanding and empathy, which would be the style of a human sensibility.

Yet (the demon critic rushes to remind me) the "action novelists" and I share the same questionable motive. We are all interested by Che *because* of his previous public existence, just as we expect our readers to be. Imagining him was to be my implication in our shared history. And this interest, as the critic suspects, feels like a violation.

The critic mentions another genre of violation, pornography. There, too, the critic says that one's interest in the work isn't "literary." Pornography, like fiction that uses characters from the public spectacle, borrows its charisma from another realm. We're fascinated—indeed hypnotized—by the subject, so we lack the inner freedom that the work of art requires in its maker and its audience. Perhaps this is to say that sex, as the critic apprehends it, is not to be talked about in literature; literature is the realm of whole people rather than parts of people. Literary characters are their sensibility, and pornographic sex is somehow, like history, outside of (before, or against) individual sensibility.

And when I read a historical novel I often have the sense of something illicit being done. What intrigues the reader, forms the intrigue with the reader, is the fascination of hearing secrets—the murmurous voice of the parents overheard by the child at night. "Buckley brings us face to face with possibilities lurking behind our real headlines," Fred Isaac of the San Francisco *Chronicle* says on the back of *See You Later, Alligator,* William Buckley's novel about Che Guevara. And, as in pornography, the secrets are told unreliably. We don't know, often can't know, whether the historical details are true, are historical. (We can't know either in pornographic writing if there really is a lover that inventive, that submissive, that magisterially controlling.) And at the worst we're being willingly conned: our excitement at the action makes us indifferent to truth of the details. (Whether Raul Castro smiles as sadistically as William Buckley describes him doing, or Kutúzov spoke in the meter that Tolstoy gives him in *War and Peace.*) The work provides the delicious pleasure of being hypnotized, of knowing that the voice telling us the secrets is unreliable, that there is no reason to believe it except the pleasure it gives you, which is in part the pleasure of submission, and a submission that we half connive in.

But if the voice is unreliable, what are we hearing secrets about? The similarity to pornography makes me think that they pertain to similarly basic instincts. For me, anyway, the prestige of the historical is the prestige of death. (At last the distinguished thing!) In historical fiction we are going backstage, being let in on "the possibilities lurking behind our real headlines"—that is to say, we get to know the working of power. But, since power grows out of the barrel of the gun (as Mao said); or since the power that creates the memory that makes the historical order possible is the right to inflict pain for debts forgotten, and so one learns not to forget (as Nietzsche imagined); or since history begins, as in Hegel's fable, when one brother is willing to die, and becomes master, and the other fears it, and becomes his slave; then the fascination with power, with history, and with the death that transfixed me in the image of Che's corpse, is, perhaps, intertwined.

To return to my demon critic for a moment, I know—and you know—that I could escape from his accusations by saying that the fabric of consciousness, that the self, is made of words. That all men and women in novels are certainly made of words. That words refer only to other words; texts depend on other texts for their meaning, and refer only to other texts, in the endless chase of "intertextuality." If both history and fiction are texts, there's no violation in crossing them, because there's no fundamental difference between the realms. So there's no obscene *fact* being illegitimately used in fiction because there's no "off stage," no outside to the text.

But I can't deny that I told a story about history because of its *particular* prestige, because it shared in the prestige of the dead body, the glamour of the corpse, its infrangible, undeniable, whispering of a transcendent truth. The true imagination of death allows one, I thought, to see the bars of the prison of one's own consciousness, and so sense its limits. Such terror lets one, as Ludwig Wittgenstein wrote, "feel the world as a limited whole—it is this that is mystical."

But Wittgenstein thought, too, that death is among those things about which we must keep silent. ("Death is not an event in life. . . . The solution of the riddle of life in space and time lies *outside* space and time.") Yet it is those things that cannot be talked about, that lie outside space and time, those things that we can't apprehend directly, that we nonetheless can't stop talking about. We speak of them in metaphors and tragic symbols, we form our humanity in how we place our-selves in relation to them. And we quarrel endlessly over what is the right relation, the true sacrament.

Sometime in our lives (the hospital waiting room, the near

miss, and perhaps in the work of tragic art) we feel that *our* life ends when our body dies, so that nature, though a tyrant, and most tyrannical in our death, is also in death what makes our life most *ours.* The imagination of death allows us to feel the precious residue not quite encompassed by any determinism; and it allows us to know that we are a body, are more (or less) than culture, to know ourselves, our creations, our speculations, as limited. Death, that most impersonal of natural events—the event that ineluctably joins us to an unnamable indifferent nature—is also what gives us our personhood.

We have our self, then, only in our continual remembrance that we will lose it, feel it as ours only as we imagine its loss. (It is in this sense that I think there is a truth hidden in the perception that the self is joined to a style of loss.) In tragic, sacramental symbols, we mark our difference from the tyranny of nature, of absolute determinism, even as we recognize its final power.

The metaphors—by which nature as death joins culture—take more than religious forms. They include men and women as self-regulating machines that process ones and *zeros;* and the individual who becomes the agent of history when he or she, as a member of the world proletariat, discovers his or her own individual *nothingness* and so joins with his or her class to act; and they include history as the destruction of the first world's cities by a third-world revolution. These metaphors open at one end towards an apprehension of emptiness—of death—and are ways that we imagine the shape of our personhood and its tasks. And the contest over these shaping metaphors is surely one basic part of history.

I told this story about history because of its particular prestige; that prestige was its opening towards death. The nourishment that I wanted from Che's corpse was to have a fruitful relation to death; to feel, through *his* death, my own person-hood. I wanted, improbably enough, to write the sort of story that makes history as the history of *individuals* possible. Of course, I knew I couldn't quite do this; I couldn't create a new gospel, or a new Athens! But, tutored by the best contemporary work—Norman Mailer's, Toni Morrison's, E. L. Doctorow's, John Barth's, Thomas Pynchon's, all come vividly to mind, exciting envy and effort—I could try to draw attention to the process of story telling, tell a story that shows and is also self-reflectively *about* the processes that (in a different forum, and with a more collective sort of authorship) make the kinds of stories that allow us to feel ourselves as individuals, as the subjects of history—stories of the destruction of gods, or the tragic heroes who are almost gods. Each story's particular form relates us, in its way, to a death which we might feel as ours; it relates us to our emptiness, and so gives us our sense of self.

Towards the end, as Che marches through the Bolivia of my novel, he learns that he no longer belongs to himself; perhaps he never did. He is the stories the Bolivian Indians have begun to make of him. Che learns from those stories, from the content of them, and from the fact of them, that we are painfully formed by others, joined each to each, as if one vein ran through all of us. That is to say, one facet of the black diamond of his transitoriness is turned to him by these stories: he is already a collective creation, without a stable essence; he is daily transformed as words in the peasants' mouths. (Knowing—and acting from the knowledge—that he is made by others, that he is their transitory creation, is Che's version of sensibility as a song of loss of self.)

In tragedy, we make up the hero that dies so that, through his death, we might feel ourselves as passing away, and so feel ourselves as irreplaceable individuals. Sometimes we forget that the hero was our collective creation, and he moves outside us—an image, or a god. In my novel, Che himself feels that collective creation as a loss of his magisterial self, feels it as suffering, and reminds us, *through his suffering,* that we make him. His apprehension of his own emptiness is that he is made by others, he is in a story that makes him up. In this, he reminds the reader who might identify with him, that we, too, are made up—given a sense of self—by the stories we collectively tell, each contributing to the creation of the other. So death (for by telling a story we change the hero, we cause his suffering) and life (for by making the hero, we gain our life) are joined in the violent, sometimes fruitful act of story telling.

In my novel, Che's work in Bolivia (as well as his bloody deeds!) is to instruct the Indians in how they are to relate themselves to his death. He tries to live and to shape his speech so that the questions he treasures will persist, so that the Indians will be impaled on his themes, his rebellious relation to *unnecessary* suffering. Che is turned into a story again by his friend Ponco, who gathers up his pieces, assembling and completing the documents that were left at his death. And again, Che is made a story by me. (Do his questions persist? Are *they* the precious residue that death sifts out?) The task of relationship to the "unspeakable," is, I think, to find the story that will allow one to be active in making and telling—and making by telling—history; that will let one know that it is history's tragic stories that shape the particular self one will have.

When I began my attempt to make history into fiction, into history *as* fiction, the corpses were mostly coming from Vietnam. History bore down on one like a juggernaut. There was then, too, an active movement against the war, bent on comprehending history, and giving it human dimensions again. Those of us involved never, I think, felt more powerful, more fully ourselves; and we were never more convinced that history was made by forces that we couldn't control. *Or worse:* If history was the war between the first world and the third then we lost either way. My imagination was haunted by specters created by a terrified ambivalence. I longed for implication in history; and I everywhichway dreaded it—a mixture of impotence and terror, of hope, and of rage.

Such feelings make one long for a god, a specter who will protect one, and justify one, and permit one the acts that seem so necessary to bring the world back under control; a specter who will make one's sacrifices meaningful, tell one how to relate to a death that matters. At so many demonstrations we chanted the names of heroes, both foreign and domestic, as if we were praying that they might be *our* heroes, our pattern, our protectors, our gods. But which—hero or god? Such leader-gods are all-too-human; instead of providing a recognition of his dying (and our dying) they (like Mao, say) demand god-like status and god-like immortality—signified to the world by the hecatombs of sacrifices offered them. Even then—as we stumbled and ran through the streets—most of us remembered and dreaded the sacrifices that have been made to such false gods. But perhaps if we—after Freud—could see the process by which the god was made we would see how our own need had made him, that he was our *metaphor.* Could that saving distance keep people from repeating horror, collaborating in slaughter?

The novel, I thought, could participate in that special sort of theogony that is not quite theogony, could show each strand of its ambivalence equally poised, show the creation and destruction of the tragic symbol, and something of the process by which we, readers and writers, actors and chorus, perform the creation. My ambivalence about joining the third world could be transformed, in the novel's drama, into an ambivalence that both creates and destroys the gods, so the novel would show, I hope, that we create them as they create us. This odd in-between state of half-knowing one created the hero, and so worshipping through the symbol one's own power would be (wherever I attained it) neither irony nor my style of ambivalence, but ambivalence grasped at the deeper level where death and life intertwine; it would be a kind of dreaming while awake.

But my novel also contains large (I hope not acrid) dollops of irony, questions I couldn't surrender or it wouldn't have been *my* novel. What if the creation even of a *hero* is blasphemy? What if Guevara is a protagonist but *not* a hero? What if Beckett is right, and all action farcically cancels itself out, the water the clown yearns for forever pulled beyond his reach, history a funhouse barrel, where people try to keep their balance while the barrel spins, but the barrel spins only because they move about trying to keep their balance? So how could my book attain the dreaming-while-awake that creates transparent tragic symbols? It remains a story *about* that dreaming; not the story of *our* hero, no matter how often his name was chanted, but still, always, a story about another people's hero. Not a story, then, of Che's third world, but of the first world, or perhaps a story of the first world as one of its citizens once upon a time wildly, erratically, ambivalently—turning and twitching in his fevered sleep—dreamed and feared and longed to join a larger community.

DEATH
AND THE
IMAGE

for Stanley Cavell

☐   In *The World Viewed,* the philosopher Stanley Cavell places Film in the volume marked Memory; for films, like memories, give us a world that is ours, yet that we are barred from entering. Memories, of course, may, on certain remarkable occasions, become vividly reborn as part of one's current telling; they enter us reincarnated, rich with anxiety and the demand that we change our lives, that we continue our narratives, in light of their questions, to a new momentary stopping point. But only some films are such inspired memories; others are that failed sort of memory called nostalgia. Nostalgia: because we think of the time we remember as a time we have survived; and, because we dream we have survived it—its challenges, its interrogations—we think we watch a history that is simply past, incapable of troubling us in the present. We are fond spectators of a calm time, lulling, purged of that constant moment-to-moment anxiety for one's survival that edges each present moment with pain. It's as if the nostalgic film (both fiction and documentary) longs to attain the status of the snapshot, the perfect form, Kodak and Polaroid reassure me, for nostalgia, the past not as question, but as possession.

I think that the continual consumption of such images-become-snapshots, in T.V. news, newspaper photos, magazine photo-essays, films, and videos, makes us feel immortal; not alive as humans once were; and, like gods, not quite capable of imagining our deaths. One figure for this in my thinking is Patty Hearst's demonic kidnappers, who, when their not-so-safe house was surrounded, stayed inside, watching themselves on T.V. as the police burned them up. I imagine they felt they couldn't really be dying because they were watching themselves on television, and so were outside the flames that consumed them. Besides, they could always change the station.

Death is the absent guest in most of the images we use to divert ourselves—not death as subject or as spectacle but felt death, our transience, our violence, and our will to end our lives. Did the artist's shaping violence form the image or do we feel that at most he shot a camera and the mechanism did the rest? We know better; every great cinematic artist teaches that each frame must be formed by the artist and by the viewer's imagination. Yet it is easy also to deceive, to make us feel that the camera, that machine, doesn't have full implication in what it records. Our entertainments are often bloody minded, but the violence is usually localized in one kill-crazy hero, rather than experienced as the force that forms the world we see on (and perhaps off) the screen. And viewers need not quite acknowledge that they, too, imagine the world in the image, and so participate in what it represents; rather, one pretends that one *sees* it. The image overwhelms the imaginative faculty, that sense, redolent with instinctual involvement, that we collaborate in making the world through our shaping violence and our love. (Imagination, that is, as opposed to fixation, when one is fixed on, impaled upon, a world simply seen.)

But we cheat ourselves, I think, when we deaden our uneasiness before death, that fiercely beseeching anxiety that is the "gift" of the death instinct. That invaluable anxiety might make us acknowledge our desire to die, and our violence, and so (if we bear it, if we do not simply repress it or deaden it) it might cause us to call on the god Eros. It might opportune our political imaginations to create a new dispensation for ourselves, one equal to the magnified means of annihilation that we have put at the service of the death instinct.

To speak of the images of the destruction of European Jewry, in the films I will write of here—*Night and Fog, Shoah, Hotel Terminus*—as if such pictures might be deadening, soothing, distracting, or nostalgic seems absurd. Yet often in considering these events, one slips into melancholy, or dark mourning, or a too insistent piety, when, if death were truly in what we imagine, one would feel, as the narrator of Alain Resnais's documentary *Night and Fog* reminds us, "endless, uninterrupted fear." What I think the filmmakers I will speak about demand of us seems almost inhuman: that the death instinct, and our anxiety, might be felt by us and in us, in each of its manifestations, that the viewer might play every role in the film: executioner, spectator, victim, and the artist whose violence forms the image of this kingdom of death. Resourceful animals, we need all exits closed or we will avoid this confrontation. The viewer must feel the death instinct operates not only in the characters but in the theme, not only in the theme but in the way the film's world was made, and in the way his or her mind operates in its understanding and enjoyment.

I do not mean, please understand me, that we are all responsible for the Holocaust. But I do think that if we cannot enter imaginatively into history—even this history, and especially this history—then our world will be a delusion, and our history a spectacle, and eventually, as the drugs wear off, an intolerable weight. In describing the cure of the neurosis, D. W. Winnicott speaks of the neurotic's first step towards cure coming when she reincludes her history, even its traumas, in the domain of infantile omnipotence. For the neurotic either represses the offending event, making the world and her personality unreal, or the trauma is experienced as an utterly external event that has crushed her. She, like us, must regain that sense the healthy infant has that her cry helps make the breast, that her desire collaborates in the creation of the world. Without this sense, half-illusory though it may be, our imagination is stunned by the inert mechanical mass of the world, incapable of creating the new dispensation we require, and we ourselves become machine-like in our pleasures or our destruction.

Each of these films begins by acknowledging the near impossibility of even representing the Holocaust. In part this is a piety; to admit that the Holocaust might be represented seems almost to deny the enormity of its horror, and its singularity. The Holocaust is, in a phrase borrowed from Rilke, "the bottle filled full of death . . . out of which people were forced to drink a bitterness of undiluted death." Impossible to represent this, for, as Freud writes, the death instinct is never simply, singly, manifested; death is always fused with eros. Or, perhaps, as the world was about to learn, not always; and then how can it be represented? We have no forms for such an unknown thing. "The problem of my film," the director of *Shoah,* Claude Lanzmann said, "was to show death." But can it be shown? For what one wishes to show does not adhere precisely in any of the documents the executioners left, any of the traces the victims made; even the survivors' voices. Those are papers; artifacts; sounds; and being adheres in each, when what the film wants to give is, precisely, non-being.

But if it could show us that blackness, we would become "frantically terrified"; death as catastrophe, death as drive—each is the signal for an anxiety beyond bearing. "If you could lick my heart," one survivor tells Lanzmann, "it would poison you." The Holocaust survivor's problem is the film's problem: death cannot be shown; it must be shown, must be felt, or all reality is drained from this world. It must, frame by frame, be remembered; it must be forgotten or life cannot continue.

"We should need the very mattress," the narrator of *Night and Fog* says as the camera pans over the dormitory at Auschwitz, "at once meat safe and strong box . . . the blanket that was fought over, the denunciations and oaths. Only the hush and shade remain of this brick dormitory." [The camera pans outside.] "Here is the setting . . . an autumn sky indifferent to everything . . . evokes a night shrill with cries. . . ." Can we hear that cry? Resnais here presents the fundamental difficulty of the Holocaust documentary as if it were a difficulty of evidence, of having the right documentation, the actual mattresses the victims slept on. As if one could believe the past only if it were no longer past, or as if documents and artifacts could return it to us (when, equally, documents, mattresses, in their very quiddity, hide non-being from us)! This is the mark of the greatest piety, and the greatest mischief. The piety: such an event should not be spoken of, cannot be spoken of; one cannot enter into the register of the historical order, of memory, what ended, or should have ended, history. And it marks the greatest evil: those who say that such a thing could not have happened.

Resnais shows us one face of the greatest evil, a still photo of a camp commandant "who pretends to know nothing. . . . How discover what remains of the reality of the camps, when it was despised by those who made them and eluded those who suffered there. . . ." [The camera pans past beds.] "Where sleep itself was a danger . . . no description, no shot can restore their true dimension, endless uninterrupted fear." What new forms, what new apprehensions, might restore our anxiety, and help us to bear it as well, not despising the events, repressing them, piously or evilly denying them—even if we must, then, also, despise ourselves?

Resnais begins by reversing the expected terms of some problems. He makes the horrible ordinary, so we might believe it; and then he makes the ordinary horrible, so that we might fear it. "An ordinary road," his film begins, "an ordinary village . . . names like any other on maps and in guide books. . . ." The camps are built, and the Jews, interned, "go on living their ordinary lives six hundred miles from home." The SS, with its registrars, Kapos, commandants, prostitutes, "managed to reconstitute the semblance of a real city." The ordinary becomes horrible—the tracks from our city of the living lead to the camp. The horrible becomes ordinary. The camp becomes a city. Not our city? Perhaps, but not, anymore, *not* our city, either.

Yet this is hardly enough to bring death into the image and into our consciousness. For that, the artist must understand the making of this city not simply as ordinary but in its deepest congruence with his own manner of making his film. For

Resnais, the most lyric of the directors I will discuss, and the finest craftsman, it is art that builds the walls of the city; our city; the camps; his film. Death is most felt not in the voices of survivors, not in still photos or documentary footage from the camps, not in the silence of nature, but in all these things only when the artist has found a way to make himself and us participate in the *building* of these images of the destruction of the Jews, and so in that limited, symbolic, so necessary way, in what the images show. We can participate, then, *symbolically* in the destruction of the Jews, and in our own destruction; for to imagine properly is also, symbolically, to perform and to suffer. The filmmaker must apprehend that the bringing of death can come from the way his sensibility operates. His sensibility, too, is what made the camps, made death, and if this were not the case, he would not, I think, be an artist, for in this manner, too, death is crucial in giving a world. One might say that each artist finds his sensibility, is given it as his, by apprehending—and bearing the knowledge that his sensibility imaginatively makes death also.

So for Resnais, the most formally elegant, the most artful and elegiac of the filmmakers I'm going to discuss, the camp is made by art and by craft: "A concentration camp is built like a grand hotel—you need contractors, estimates—

"The camps come in many styles: [shots of guard towers accompany this list] Swiss, Garage, Japanese, No style." Whereas for Claude Lanzmann, the director of *Shoah,* the Final Solution is a matter of methodical, step by step engineering, for Resnais, it's a matter of art; as we come to the entrance to Auschwitz, the narrator says, "The leisurely architects plan the gates no one will enter more than once."

Within those crafted gates, some prisoners are classified as "Night and Fog," a piece of Hitler's poetry; the Jews were to disappear into the night and fog, their fate forever unknown. Poetry—art and craft—made the camp; poetry—art and craft—makes Resnais's response to the camp, its representation. Poetry is complicit with death—with the real death of the camp, and with what makes the representation of the camp. If Resnais's art did not openly display this complicity it would distance him and us from the camp, turn us into spectators, and the camp into spectacle.

In the Talmud, it is asked, how, now that the Temple is destroyed, are we to make sacrifices? And why, now that the Temple is destroyed, do we study in such detail how sacrifices were made there? The sages answer that our way of making a sacrifice at the Temple is, of course, *to study* how the sacrifice had been made, to sacrifice one's lives briefly through study, in remembering the sacrifice, remembering it meticulously, step by step. In this way we symbolically enact sacrifice; our own detailed delineation, which calls upon all our powers of imagination and interpretation, both describes and is symbol for the sacrifice. The manner, that is to say, of a true representation is where the activity of representation itself is a symbolic equivalent for the act to be represented. Such symbolic sacrifices are not bloodless, not without scars; and it is a dangerous philistinism not to appreciate that the death instinct truly operates in the symbolic sacrifice as well as in the literal one.

So "arts and crafts" here make the way death is represented and the way literal death is carried out: "Each camp has its surprises: a symphony; a zoo [we see a bear]; hothouses; Goethe's oak. . . ." Resnais then shows, using still photos—using film to animate the still—the roll call of naked prisoners; the piles of the dead; the lashings and the gallows. And then adds: "The mind works on. They [the prisoners] make spoons, boxes, marionettes . . . while they hide notes, dreams." Art also entwines life with death, making the unbearable momentarily tolerable. (Is there anywhere art is not present, not formative?) The film then takes us to the hospital, a place for prisoners to be mocked with paper bandages—props, one might say—or murdered medically. We see footage in color, from present time, a shot of empty rooms. The camera then pans across black and white stills of patients. Or so one thinks, until an eye blinks. One thinks (forced to a telling misapprehension): so it wasn't a photo (though, of course it is). If motion pictures–become–snapshots describe nostalgic images, then here nostalgia is defeated by momentarily making the moving picture seem like a still, and then the slight motion of the patient's eye makes a mournful scene horrifying. Death enters because we had felt protected, because we had thought we were looking at a still, at history that had already happened. Outside history's narrative, we did not have to participate in its forward motion. But because the man will die, because he has been returned for a moment to life, we try to grasp him at the edge of the precipice; and feel our failure, and await death, again, with him.

The hospital, the narrator says, "is set-up and scenes." What is behind them? "Useless operations, amputations." Set-up and scenes, as in a film. And a crematorium, too, can be a set—a work of art that is a lie. "An incinerator can be made to look like a picture postcard. Later—today—tourists have themselves photographed in them." Beware, then, of settings and set. Beware of picture postcards, backdrops, photo opportunities, snapshots. Beware, this artist says, of art; it might make you nostalgic; it might make you a spectator; it might help you forget; and it might help you commit murder. Beware of arts and crafts. "Nothing is lost . . . women's hair" [a lovely shot of masses of hair, almost abstract in composition, until we might forget for its beauty what we are looking at] "is made into cloth, 15 pfennigs a kilo." Bones, "for manure." "Bodies . . . there's nothing left to say." [Shot of chopped off heads.] ". . . Bodies were meant for soap. As for skin . . ." [—the film shows images painted on skin. That is to say: *we watch images of images painted on skin.*]

Then: "Nothing distinguished the gas chamber from an ordinary block. What looked like a shower room welcomed the arrivals. The doors were closed. A watch was kept. The only sign—but you have to know—is the ceiling scored by fingernails." Why, I wondered, after all the horror we have seen, does the narrator add, "but you have to know"? Clearly, this moment has engrossed Resnais's imagination, for hands scraping stone is an image that will recur in his *Hiroshima, Mon Amour,* where the lover repeatedly scars her own hand by dragging her fingers against a cellar wall. The image must have spoken precisely *to him,* to his sense of himself and his project. I felt almost as if Resnais was defining himself by responding to an image in Rilke's essay "In Regard to Art." Art, Rilke says, is "the sensuous possibility of new worlds and time. . . . The artist is a dancer whose movements are broken by the constraints of his cell. That which finds no expression in his steps and limited swing of his arms comes in exhaustion from his lips, or else he has to scratch the unlived lines of his body into the walls with his wounded fingers." Art, for Rilke, is eros, sensuousness not yet able to be born, blocked by the recalcitrant unreadiness of history. But art, too, built these camps as well as their sensuous representation. Is there art then in the marks the victims' fingers made in *these* walls? Is this the end of art, or its grim mockery, or what defeats it—its hidden residue? Those who love art must stop, here, in stunned wonder. Are these markings ugly? beautiful? sublime? Here are the dancers; the unlived lines; the wounded fingers. ". . . but you have to know."

Resnais's film concludes that the Nazis' arts and crafts, "[t]he skill of the Nazis[,] is child's play today. . . . There are those who take hope again as the image fades, as though there were a cure for the scourge of these camps. . . . Those who pretend all this happened only once at a certain time and at a certain place. Those who refuse to look around them Deaf to the endless cry." Art made the camps, and their representation, and art, too, can be used to uncover that endless cry which is perhaps now also the truth of the world art sometimes makes—a cry revealed by art that may destroy art. Is this art's point of reversal, where art creates for itself a world where art can no longer exist—where "the sensuous possibility of a new world and time" becomes the sensuous embodiment of no world, and no time? Will it destroy the telling if we hear the cry, know of the marks? Perhaps. Art must be, from now on, poised on a knife's edge, aware of its own blandishments, its dangerous penchant for deception, its implication in catastrophe. *Night and Fog* provides, I think, both the sense of danger, and the program for Resnais's later fictional meditations. Film must now take on the task of warning us about art, must become a self-examining instrument, philosophical towards itself, uncovering through its representations and its manner of representing its own implications in the horror it reveals, and in the forgetting of that horror, uncovering again that final null point of art that may destroy art—the cry itself, the marks scratched in the wall.

In contrast to Resnais's elegiac and piercing tones in *Night and Fog,* Claude Lanzmann's *Shoah* seems more the work of an engineer than an artist—or the artist as an engineer. Lanzmann is literal-minded. Everything said must be shown. If Filip Müller, survivor of Birkenau and Auschwitz, an engaging man of almost preternatural self-possession, describes marching to work at the crematoria, Lanzmann shows the path with hand-held camera, as if walking it. Literal-minded here often means both boring- and bloody-minded, the combination forming, very intentionally I think, Lanzmann's equivalent for the "the banality of evil." Lanzmann means, I think, to be banal in his artistic means, inhibited in his visual vocabulary; zoom shots and pans with little variety in camera angle (usually overhead shots) make up most of his repertory. He is maddeningly compulsive in his repetition of sequences: the pan (over the former site of the camp, the surrounding forests, the Ruhr valley); the shot of the train crossing in front of the camera; the train arriving at Auschwitz; all are numbingly reshown.

From moment to moment there is little new to look at in *Shoah*. We hear of the location of the gas chamber at Treblinka, and we see bricks and snow. A survivor describes the construction of the crematoria and we see bricks and snow. A former SS officer speaks of the "undressing room" with its deceptive signs about cleanliness and work. But we see bricks and snow. Until, from a desire for variety our imagination becomes complicit in the process and we make the camp arise from the stones. We project upon the screen's projections, and now bricks and snow fill one with horror. (Over and over the same scene in the consulting room; the therapist's impassive face; his poorly chosen tie. We repeat the same story over and over, as we lie, like a corpse, on the couch, until our imagination, perhaps in part from boredom, from a desire for variety, projects a past on this meager screen.)

Literal-minded, bloody-minded, Lanzmann asks his infor-

mants, Was the path the gas vans went down paved? Or: How
did the train get from here to there? Were the trains pushed
the last kilometers into the camp? (Literal-minded, bloody-
minded, he must walk that part of the way.) Was the train
track inside the camp, or outside? He goes over the track with
a train engineer. And from here to the camps was how far?
"Here," he says, "was the Polish part, and here death." In this
concentration on detail, on process, Lanzmann seems very
much the obsessive; as if, if the right careful rituals were
followed, death might be isolated in one part. But his obses-
sion is too profound, too complete, too tireless, and soon death
spills over, here and everywhere, for if the tracks go *there,*
then they also can go *here.*

How were the gas chambers built? we hear Lanzmann's
voice asking the SS man Suchomel. Who built them? What
was their capacity? (Jewish survivors, Suchomel thinks, tend
to exaggerate it.) Lanzmann's voice asks for more details on
the precise location of the undressing area, the gas, the crematoria. As we listen to these voices we see a van drive up outside
Suchomel's house with a large antenna on top. We enter the
van and see a technician focusing Suchomel's image on a
television screen. On the T.V. screen, we hear and see Lanzmann lie to Suchomel, telling the SS officer that his face won't
be shown, his name won't be used. Reassured, Suchomel,
using a long pointer and a wall chart, describes the layout of
the camp. "I don't see," Lanzmann said later, to an interviewer, "why I should keep my word to these people. Did they
keep their word? I refuse to enter the psychology of the Nazis.
I decided to have only technical conversations." But throughout the film this choice pushes Lanzmann farther beyond
ordinary probity than such transparently poor self-justifica-
tion; in fact, what he achieves is a kind of *necessary* near-

identification with the Nazis. He, *like them,* will lie. He, like them, will, *in his way,* kill. "How could I stand this, not to jump at [Suchomel] and kill him?" he says to an interviewer. "This was not at all my purpose. My purpose was to kill him with a camera." He, like them, is only interested in technical conversations; he, like them, wishes to make the Final Solution an engineering problem.

"I refuse," Lanzmann says, "to enter the psychology of the Nazis. I decided to have only technical conversations." Instead of why—and what answer would we accept here?—we have how. But in an age when psychology is what makes souls, to substitute (as Lanzmann does) how for why—is to seem oneself the soulless, the repetitive, the machine. How far from ramp to camp? "Four kilometers." "Was the road paved?"

The victims, too, wonder *how* such a thing might be done. "We were like stones, we couldn't mention what had happened to the wife," Abraham Bomba says. "Nobody is anymore alive. How could they gas so many people at once? But they had their way how to do it. . . . It was impossible to believe that just a minute . . . before you were part of a family, you were part of a wife, a husband. Now all of a sudden, everything is dead." When the mind is stunned by what the mind can do, one asks not why but how, by what techniques, can we do such things. So this machine makes us into machines:

> I looked around me [Filip Müller says]. There were hundreds of bodies, all dressed. Piled with the corpses were suitcases, bundles, and scattered everywhere, strange, bluish purple crystals. I couldn't understand any of it. It was like a blow on the head, as if I'd been stunned. . . . Above all, I couldn't understand how they managed

to kill so many people at once. . . . Suddenly an SS man
rushed up and told me . . . "Go stir the bodies!" What
did he mean, "Stir the bodies"? . . . At that point I was
in shock, as if I'd been hypnotized, ready to do whatever
I was told. I was so mindless, so horrified, that I did
everything. . . . So the ovens were fed. . . .

Lanzmann, stunned, refuses to enter the Nazis' psychology,
to grant them inwardness. But this is, of course, the terrifying
double-bind that Hitlerism, perhaps all racism, confronts us
with. He will not be like the Nazis; they must be utterly alien
to him; they cannot even be imagined, granted insides; they
are not human. But the Nazis knew better than us the techniques of making their opponents *not human!* And so the
machine has made him into a machine; he has become like
them, for not to grant others inwardness means not to have
it oneself. His outrage, his obsessive defense ("I decided to
have only technical conversations"), meant to ensure that he
remain uncontaminated, instead brings about the very thing
he *seemingly* wants to avoid.

Lanzmann's *impersonation* is so complete that we begin to
make equivalence after equivalence: the gas vans used at
Chelmno are, one survivor has told us, like the green vans one
sees delivering cigarettes in Israel, are like, one supposes, the
vans we saw drive up to Suchomel's apartment. The SS lured
the Jews with lies (and, one must add, unlike Lanzmann,
forced them with unparalleled brutality). Lanzmann deceives
Suchomel and traps him in the van. No, not him—one must
remind oneself—*his image.* Near the beginning of the film a
survivor is shown a forest in Israel—why, one wonders, would
Lanzmann bother with this, instead of simply showing him

the original forest? It is, the survivor agrees, something like the forest in Ponari where the Jews were burned. We then pan, at high angle, a forest at Sobibor. "That's the charm of our forests: silence and beauty," a Pole, Jan Piwonski, says. "But . . . there was a time when it was full of screams . . . and that period . . . is engraved on the mind of those who lived here then." This forest is like that forest . . . these vans are like those vans that deliver cigarettes. Our half-fare railroad tickets for children are like the pricing policies used by the Nazis for the deportations. This train station is like that train station. Here are suitcases, like the suitcases that the dead left after they were "processed." The dead were called puppets; shit; bricks; rags. This is like that: metaphor, the trope which gives value, that makes a world, here destroys it by yoking our present with the kingdom of death. Through metaphor our world is unmade; replaced by another.

There is little new to look at in this film because it is not the new that interests Lanzmann but the eruption of the past. Lanzmann's method is the creation of transference, new editions, as Freud called it, of old conflicts; the sudden, almost epiphanic emergence of the spectral past to obliterate or reshape the present in its own image; in this case, to turn the apparent life of the present into the death that was the past; to kill the present, until this forest in Israel *is* for a moment that forest in Poland. Transference teaches a new lexicon: A river = a sewer for ground bones; stones = corpses; trees = deceptive propaganda to hide a killing ground; shoes = corpses; suitcases = corpses; clothing = corpses; rags = corpses; a field = a sorting place for dead people's clothing; shit = corpses; puppets = corpses; bricks = corpses; workers = cogs in a killing machine; to process = to kill people. And, of course, I must add film to this lexicon: when the Nazis rounded up the Jews of Corfu a survivor says that many gentiles came to watch. The subtitle says "for the show," but the survivor has actually said "pour le cinéma." Lanzmann makes us mad with analogies that annihilate the present: we are silent in the theater, politely not interrupting, as if we were good Germans; afraid to scream, as if we were prisoners, stunned like Müller into stirring the bodies; we look towards the flickering light, as if we were prisoners in the gas vans. And we will emerge at the end, like the survivor of the Warsaw ghetto, the last Jew on earth, stunned now by life as the others had been by death, shocked to find that "In Aryan Warsaw, life went on as naturally, and normally as before. The cafés operated normally, the restaurants, buses and streetcars . . . were open."

When Lanzmann's necessary, difficult, arduous techniques bear their bitter invaluable fruit, all these equivalences, and all the boredom and repetition, become ways of making the moments of transference bloom into a continuous transference neurosis. To accomplish this, Lanzmann, like a good analyst, is unfailingly dogged; and he is not (on rare occasions) beyond a little artifice. For Abraham Bomba, a Jewish survivor who had worked at Treblinka cutting hair, Lanzmann finds a barbershop, though he doesn't mention in the film that Bomba is now long retired. (Resnais, whose quarry is art itself, would have reminded us that this is a set, a setting.) We see Bomba working on a man's hair—but not actually; the scissors cut air; or the man, by the end of the scene, would have had no hair. The Nazis used actual barbers at Treblinka to deceive the women about to be gassed, so the victims "could sit and not get the idea that this is their last way or the last time they are going to live or breathe or know what is going on." The barbers were a piece of art on the Nazis' part: to make the Jews think that they were still part of a human community, not animals being shorn of hair to make clothing and pillows for the Wehrmacht. Bomba, speaking somewhat impassively, says that the barbers tried "to do the best we could—to be the most human we could." Lanzmann, seemingly still the obsessive engineer, doesn't, at first, ask him how he felt about this, or what he thought, but how the gas chamber looked, and where, in relation to the gas chambers, he was standing when he performed the haircuts. Bomba begins to answer and then insists, "We know already that there is no way of going out from this room, because this room was the last place they went in alive and they will never go out alive again." Lanzmann then asks again, as if that fact were not at issue, or not of interest, that Bomba tell him what the room looked like. "Can you describe precisely?" And "You cut with what—with scissors?" And "There were no mirrors?" And "Can you imitate how you did it?" And: "Where did you wait [for the next group to arrive]?" And: "You cut the hair of how many women in one batch?" *Then* Lanzmann asks Bomba, "What was your impression the first time you saw these naked women arriving with children? What did you feel?"

Bomba's reply is in every way extraordinary. First, he reminds us that "it was very hard to feel anything, because working there day and night between dead people, between bodies, your feeling disappeared, you were dead." But then he says, "As a matter of fact, I want to tell you something that happened." *As a matter of fact*—and what he has been telling us previously have not quite been facts, for something has been screened out of them—he tells us that he knew many of the women whose hair he cut, yet he could not tell them anything of what awaited them. He begins to speak, as patients often will (or those in severe psychological trouble, or artists), not of himself, but of a double, a barber who recognizes among his "clients" his wife and sister. Then: "I can't. It's too horrible. Please." Bomba weeps.

The dialogue that follows between Lanzmann (offscreen) and Bomba (in a barber's smock, with a mirror behind him, standing over a man in a barber chair) is reminiscent of Beckett's tramps, or a director and an actor, or of any patient and any therapist:

"We have to do it. You know it."
"I won't be able to do it."
"You have to do it. I know it's very hard. I know, and I apologize."
"Don't make me go on please."
"Please. We must go on."

Bomba, crying, finishes his story. "They could not tell them this was the last time they stay alive, because behind them was the German Nazis, SS men, and they knew that if they said a word, not only the wife and the women, who were dead already, but also they would share the same thing with them. In a way they tried to do the best for them with a second longer, a minute longer, just to hug them and kiss them, because they knew they would never see them again."

Bomba is right, of course. In a machine world, stunned, half-hypnotized, it is very hard to have a feeling. Lanzmann has asked us, impelled us, through his incessant repetition of scenes, the film's long silences, the pauses for translations, the obsessive attention to details, to enter boredom, that fake death, like the psychoanalytic patient, that fake corpse on the couch. The boring details have given us the sense that we have the freedom to look away, when really we are hypnotized by the repetition of actions, the familiarity, only to find that the repetition has lulled us, the affectlessness has allowed for an eruption of feeling, and we, along with Bomba, are—to use the Nazis' word—*transported,* transported back to the camp. Bomba then incarnates the past. He reads the memory traces inscribed on his body; he enacts the kinetic memories, relives the event. (Poetry, here, is the marks the prison made in the dancer's body.)

One of the SS men interviewed, assistant Nazi head of the Warsaw ghetto, says to Lanzmann, "We're reaching no new conclusions."

Lanzmann says, "I don't think we can."

But Lanzmann doesn't want new conclusions, he wants the old ones revived. And perhaps some resonance of the Holocaust has unknowingly scarred us as well, for sometimes, through identification, or because of something we find in ourselves, we, too, accompany Lanzmann's subjects. To bring about transference, Lanzmann has played the part of fellow victim and of Nazi. Like the therapist, he has impersonated both the ego's ally, and the monstrous figure from the past, so he might guide Bomba and the others to go back, to enter death again. "To accompany the dead," Lanzmann called it in an interview. "To resurrect them. And to make them die a second time, but to die with them."

Or almost. Filip Müller tells this story:

The violence climaxed when they tried to force the people to undress. A few obeyed, only a handful. Most of them refused to follow the order. Suddenly, like a chorus, they all began to sing. The whole "undressing room" rang with the Czech national anthem, and the Hatikvah. That moved me, terribly. . . . That was happening to my coun-

trymen, and I realized that my life had become meaningless. Why go on living? For what? So I went into the gas
chamber with them, resolved to die. With them. Suddenly, some who recognized me came up to me. . . . A
small group of women approached. They looked at me
and said, right there in the gas chamber . . . "So you want
to die. But that's senseless. Your death won't give us back
our lives. That's no way. You must get out of here alive,
you must bear witness to our suffering, and to the injus-
tice done to us."

This reprieve—we're just reprieved corpses, one of the Jewish camp workers had told a Kapo—is not, precisely, a cause
for rejoicing. If Müller is willing to die with them—as the
movie asks us to die with them—he is granted life again. But
only if he accepts the task they, the dead, offer him, and that
task is to remember more than he knows he can remember,
to show more than he can say, to enact for others, over and
over, their entry into the gas chamber, his desire to die, their
death, his reprieve; he is spared if he is willing to make his life
an abreaction, an incarnation of their dying, if he allows death
to be endlessly reborn in him. Müller's story warns me, too,
of one of the costs of the tradition represented by the Talmud's
injunction to repeat in the ritual of study the activities of the
dead. Such an incarnation may require the help of others, but
it may also annihilate the present that one shares with them.
Perhaps that's why Lanzmann found the work of making
Shoah so isolating, why, in addition to the carnage that surrounded them, several of the survivors speak of having this
same thought: that if they survived, they would be the last Jew
left alive.

. . .

Lanzmann's technique is the inducement of transference; at whatever cost—even if it obliterates the present—the past must live in us. Marcel Ophüls's film *Hotel Terminus,* produced by his company, Memory Pictures, might be compared to that aspect of analysis that aims for knowledge. Patient and analyst methodically analyze repressions, not to bring about a reconnection between the ego and its stores of buried feeling, but so that one might accurately know the past again, and confront a present that, though bitter, is purged of distortions.

Ophüls's film, his analysis, traces the hidden—repressed, one might say—career of Klaus Barbie, the Nazi torturer of Lyon, murderer of Jews and resistance leaders, who was used and protected by the American government after the war. The neurotic—or historical actors—have, from Ophüls's point of view, disorders of memory. The neurotic tells the story of his life with the parts in the wrong order; or with gaps; or he contradicts himself; and he denies or distorts the reality of anything he sees in the present that might challenge his fantastical past. Eventually he becomes incoherent. The neurotic cannot remember, for example, that, after the war, he recruited the Nazi torturer Klaus Barbie to work for U.S. intelligence. He cannot remember if he knew that Barbie was a torturer, or how he avoided knowing. Or he cannot remember if he collaborated with the Nazis, or made false papers for the resistance. The neurotic cannot remember if, when he worked as a bellboy at the Hotel Terminus, he saw the SS officers bring suspects through the lobby in handcuffs. He cannot remember if, at the police station where he worked, he heard people scream. He cannot remember if he saw the Jewish children being deported. "Did I say that?" the U.S. agent, Kolb, says in this film. "Then I was wrong in my memory." Ophüls reads to the U.S. agent Taylor his own memo calling Barbie a Nazi idealist, and asks what "idealist" means, as we look at a picture of Barbie's eyes. "I don't know. I wish I could rewrite that today." ("Perhaps," Ophüls says, with mild, characteristic cruelty, "especially today.") Madame Hammerle, a collaborator, says she saw the death camps in "propaganda films." Such exaggerated, impossible to believe events! Ophüls asks, "Propaganda films? Was that *Night and Fog?*" But Hammerle can't recall that, either. Wolfgang Gustmann, a former SS officer, thought Barbie was a "fantastic guy"; as for talk of Nazi crimes, it's "time to be done with it." The massacre at Oradour? "I'm still not sure what happened . . . if such a thing really happened." The deportation of Jews, the Final Solution? "Maybe we'd like a pact of silence about some things."

Because of what one knows but doesn't want to know, there are soon many related matters one must distort or avoid—without knowing, of course, that one is avoiding them. Kolb didn't know the resistance leader Jean Moulin had died under Barbie's torture, or even that he had died. Or that he was really a resistance leader. "I knew Moulin was a resistance fighter or something like that," Kolb says. Ophüls, an amiable but tenacious interrogator, presses him, "Why do you say something like that?" "Well, I'm a political scientist, so I like to know what the fellow's orientation is." He means, of course, as neurotics often do, the reverse of what he says: he doesn't want to know what a person's political orientation is, or even that the person existed. The neurotic devises strategies of disingenuous denial. Kolb says, "[Barbie] didn't strike me as the sort of person who would need to torture." Or as Gustmann, the former SS officer says, using a vicious kind of magical thinking, Barbie couldn't have been that sort of person, because dogs liked him. Forced to admit his crimes, Barbie's allies must make torture not matter, because those

Barbie murdered were communists, and thus not resistance fighters but "something like that," and, really, enemies. Besides, the accounts were undoubtedly exaggerated.

Ryan, the State Department lawyer who was forced to confront the charge that the United States might have employed Barbie, says "controlled ignorance is still ignorance." Actually, it's not; it's repression. Such repression requires scrupulous avoidance of knowledge: Kolb denies he knew about the trial of Hardy, the man accused of betraying Moulin, for if he had, he would have learned that Barbie, his prize agent, had tortured resistance members. Kolb and his superiors say they only read the army paper, *Stars and Stripes.* Like Omrcamin, the Vatican official who collaborated with the United States in smuggling Barbie out of Europe, they followed "the Catholic principle, no questions asked." (Besides, Omrcamin says, there are Jews with immense riches, "who are vengeful and fabricate crimes to accuse Barbie of.")

Those collaborating with Barbie, using him and being used by him, must either have known with whom they collaborated, or must have particularly not wanted to know, which is, psychoanalytically, the same—for how do you know what you want to repress unless you know it? So for those engaged in repression, self-deception, and deception of others, the great luxury—reserved for psychotics and those at the pinnacles of power—is to be "out of the loop," to have what one wishes happen, without knowing about it. "Do what you have to do," the head of the U.S. Army intelligence service says, "but keep me out of trouble."

"I've forgotten," Barbie says. "If they haven't, it's their problem." But Barbie, who is not simply a liar but, more disastrously, a cause of lies told by others, is the corrosive principle itself. In this he is reliable: everything he says, as in this last remark, is backwards. Their problem, our problem, is that we have forgotten. What those with power do not want to remember is, of course, what Barbie did at the Hotel Terminus. In Lanzmann's movie we see trains arriving at the death camps, over and over; in Ophüls's film, we see elevator doors closing in front of an opulently decorated floor of a prosperous hotel. What went on behind those doors—obscene? It's impossible to see, but not impossible to know—in fact, one can easily know, if one wishes. Behind those doors Barbie walked through his domain, looking at a floor littered with those torture victims too weak to stand anymore. He picked up their faces with the tip of his boot, and if the face looked Jewish to him, he crushed it. (We learn this just after Kolb has told us Barbie was not anti-Semitic.) Women had their backs broken, their hands and arms put into manacles with spikes pointing into the flesh. Victims were given "ice baths," the water poured from an old tin container. They were beaten. (As one victim says, "I passed out a respectable number of times.") Torture, and death, and deportation of Jews is what is not seen, and, again, though we can know it, we can—like the victim's bed whose absence is lamented in *Night and Fog*—no longer precisely see it. But Barbie's effects can be seen, not simply the marks he left on the victims' bodies, but the effects wrought by denying how much of our world is still connected to that once luxurious hotel. For after so much evasion, the neurotic begins to make mistakes in the present, and soon forgets what to call things anymore. As Barbie's daughter says, "I can't exactly say what a National Socialist is." And Barbie, deported from Bolivia under guard, feels he can safely challenge an interrogator: "Can you explain what Nazi means?"

Fear of communism and, in most of the collaborators, hatred of the Jews, made them ally themselves with Barbie, and Ophüls pays due attention to their motives. But it is the effects that concern Ophüls—how a once shared world has been corroded till the meaning of words, of symbols, of feelings, is confused, distorted, lost. The multiform, exfoliating denials soon seem part of a deeper, wider, darker forgetting of the Holocaust itself, as if our everyday actions, our comfort, our ease (who is putting us at our ease?), even our prosperity—based in part on a war machine that did perhaps, as the defeated Nazis wished, "continue east"—might perhaps be a way of forgetting. The documentary's job is to put elements back in their proper place, but not so much to rebuild a present—something outside the strength of even the best analyst—as to show that this world we take for real, of amiable billiard games, cards, of beer and ease, camaraderie, fellowship, cognac and brandy snifters, Lenten masks, Christmas ornaments and what we think they stand for, doesn't, in fact, anymore quite exist. Like a good analyst, Ophüls uses forcefully put questions or well chosen quotations from our past, or rapid editing that brusquely points out contiguous matters strangely overlooked or denied. Ophüls's constantly inquiring camera darts over the subject's shoulder to his shelves, or into the filmmaker's archives, bringing related or seemingly disparate elements into the frame. His editing montages the truth, as when Kolb's mild assessment of Barbie is put over Christmas tree ornaments, and then beside the accounts of those he tortured. It is easy, of course, to surrender one's faith in nation states or in the U.S. intelligence community, and perhaps even in religion, but the corrosions linked to Barbie seemed to me both deeper and more widespread than that, and I soon felt as if, if I continued to believe in the blandishments of patriotism or radicalism, if I continued to accept the comforting illusion that the world of neighborliness, of home, of friendship and loyalty existed when that is so rarely the case, then I would destroy even that world's possibility.

At one point, Kolb, a virtuoso of denial, tries to save our American amour propre by denying that Barbie was a torturer. In the process Kolb helps destroy morality. He reassures himself that Barbie was so skillful an interrogator that he wouldn't need to torture. With impressive worldliness, Kolb adds that this does not mean that Barbie was a decent man. "There's a world of difference between intelligence," Kolb instructs us, "and high moral standards, and the ability to manipulate people—which is what intelligence work is about." It is a chilling moment in the film, not because what it reveals about the world is so awful, or for what it says about Kolb, whom one has long ago begun to despise. One's discomfort goes deeper. You see, Kolb is saying, I, too, am a professional of interrogation—it's not that I have some moral objection to torture, the world is now far too cynical, too sophisticated for moral objections. And you, Mr. Ophüls, as a man of the world, wouldn't accept such moral objections anyway—you, Mr. Ophüls, are an artist, too, an artist of interrogation, so you understand that one might be against torture aesthetically (for no other standards exist). Torture is unprofessional; it lacks an economy of means; excessive force is ugly. (If others, one might say, think too much of the shared world still exists, Kolb thinks that wisdom is to deny that any of it exists. Or as he puts it, with contented despair, "The whole world is shot through with moral ambiguities.") So Barbie, Kolb says, wouldn't have used torture. He would, like you, Mr. Ophüls, have been a better manipulator of people and of images, of the image of himself, and of the world, and taken you out for a few beers and bratwurst, as I would have done, as in fact I did with Barbie, when I interrogated him on whether he was guilty of torture, and as we often see you do with your victims in this film. And so Barbie would put his subject at his ease, as you do with your subjects—and your film (Kolb might have said) is filled with images of ease, of after dinner liqueurs, of subjects at their favorite billiard tables or by their swimming pools. (Who is putting us at our ease?)

Kolb is telling us of Barbie's genius as an interrogator, but he indicts Ophüls, too. I recognize myself in the style of Kolb's far from foolish cynicism, so, though I despise him, I cannot simply ignore his indictment. And, as I have identified with Ophüls, thinking that Ophüls's position was a protected and innocent one, Kolb speaks of me as well. Resnais is an artist who finds art in the making of the death camps; Lanzmann is an obsessive engineer, who methodically rebuilds the camps; and Ophüls—how could I have ignored this?—is, like Barbie, an interrogator, a man after information.

But, again, the specific cure for the death brought into reality by Barbie's methods, is Ophüls's methods, their modeling of a therapeutic use of the death instinct to find, again, correct information, and to make this representation. Of course, Ophüls is no torturer, yet he even, quite pointedly, causes psychological pain to some of those he interviews. We watch Ophüls, for example, talking to a colleague about a man he will film, as the man, Barbie's South American assistant, waits in another room, being filmed as he fidgets and waits. Ophüls remarks that the man must be squirming by now, and we cut to him squirming. Polk, a German who worked for U.S. intelligence, says, worriedly, "This film won't be shown in Germany, will it?" Polk desperately fears "repercussions." Ophüls reminds Polk, a seemingly weak and insecure man, that he has already signed a release; Polk blanches; shudders;

shrinks within himself. It is not simply that Ophüls, unlike Lanzmann, will not play the Nazi liar. Rather, he has a different role to play. Ophüls, like Barbie, is good at manipulating people; his subjects say more than they mean to, and their discomfort is one of his tools. In this film we often look at still photos of resistance leaders and politicians and Nazis, but when we move into close-ups of these photos, it is only the torturers whose eyes are shown. Torturers have eyes, and viewers, like ourselves, have eyes (for we, too, are after information), and so the question is not, can we be innocent, or can we avoid our own violence, for death here, too, will form the world of information; the question is what sort of tormentors will we be? Like Barbie or like Ophüls?

But what kind of interrogator is this Ophüls? There is a scene in the first half of the movie that spoke to me of Ophüls's character in this film, and that persona is, I think, one of the film's most striking creations. Ophüls is speaking with Monsieur Zuchner, who, as police chief of Lyon, sometimes interceded with the SS on behalf of French citizens, and sometimes, perhaps, collaborated. In any case, like many of those Ophüls interviews, he is uneasy, and has surrounded himself with books and papers that he hopes will document his good works. Ophüls, if not positively gleeful, smiles broadly, far from indifferent to Zuchner's unease. Zuchner speaks of those he helped, including the son of the man who owns the Bel cheese company. We see for a moment the familiar emblem of the company, La Vache qui Rit, the Laughing Cow. The innocent emblem curdles as I watch it, another small reminder now of the Occupation, of the manifold forms that collaboration takes, and I think, Well, the Laughing Cow hasn't heard the bad news yet. Zuchner is proud not only that he interceded for a French citizen, but, more particularly, for a powerful man's son. Ophüls laughs, and says, "Perhaps there are times, not just in wartime, when it's better to be rich and famous than not rich and famous," and I thought, that's a remark worthy of Lear's fool. Zuchner smiles at Ophüls and agrees, not quite realizing what he's agreeing to. In a small way, as in *King Lear,* such remarks restore a knowable world for us, with continuities that, though painful, are almost bearable. The fool won't allow us to live in a world of lies. He laughs at us as we try to squirm away from the past and its errors, contort ourselves to protect our wounded dignity, attempt to cover ourselves with hypocrisy or, as in Kolb's case or Edmund's, with cynicism. When the king is stripped of his protections, lost in the emptiness of the bitter present, the fool may give him a piece of the world, a refurbished truism become a timeless truth. But can we bear that, either?

Barbie, deported from Bolivia, on his way to the airport, says, "Only the winner can speak." We know, then, that *this* truism must be the reverse of the truth; so, only the loser is given speech. For the winner is power, propaganda, the unreal world of ideology. Those, like Verges, Barbie's lawyer, a petty demon who has the audacity to say he sees himself as defending the individual against state power, are, in their self-deception (or their lies) particularly dangerous, for they, too, are really cogs in some power machine's ideology. (Ophüls briefly interviews Claude Lanzmann about Verges. Lanzmann says, devastatingly—for we know how much horror *Shoah* has acknowledged—"I don't understand lawyers.") We can be, it would seem, part of the awful grinding machinery of history, or victims of that machinery, or taking our modern image-anodynes we can, though both part of the machinery *and* its victims, dream that we are only spectators. The novel, my own blessed form, has many times specialized in making a triumph of such defeats. Accepting that there is no alternative to the machinery of the state, many novels teach that we might at best be willing victims, those who love their fate, prodigies of suffering, heroes and heroines of sensibility. But Ophüls has, I think, remembered another path: We can be, like him, fools. The fool does not deny death, either his own catastrophe, or his violence. He tells the truth to power, tells Lear that he lives in an imaginary world, provoking Lear's rage, not only for his truths, but because the fool is often, and intentionally, mean, capable of sorrow over Lear's naked state, but also amused by it. He won't allow evasions, and insists on getting everything right. (Everything about the past, that is. At one point in the film, Ophüls cannot remember the current date.) The trick of the fool's survival is, in part, that he lacks pomp; apparently unthreatening to all, and so tolerated by those he will mockingly undo. Ophüls, a shaggy, amiable man, has great integrity, but little dignity. Denied an interview with the Nazi Bartlemus, he walks through a garden looking for Bartlemus under cabbage leaves, until a housewife, evoking the sanctity of private property, shoos him away. (A good analyst would also, one assumes, be similarly lacking in dignity, for pomp is based on a denial that the way up is the way down, on denying, for example, that the accumulation of money satisfies the infant's desire to accumulate his powerful shit.) The fool and the analyst are the curative forms of the torturer, the way that the death instinct might be used to overcome the death instinct that is embodied in repression. And, like a good analyst, the fool reminds us of some truths, some almost unbearable continuities between our lives and our parents' lives.

The fool, and the analyst, know that only if the false world is properly and thoroughly destroyed, not nihilistically but slowly, meticulously, piece by piece; and only if one acknowledges its destruction, and so the destruction of one's false self, can the world given by the past be even in part returned to you. I am reminded here of one of the analyst D. W. Winnicott's patients, who had developed a "false self" to please her mother, her lovers, her friends. When her false sense of herself and the world was undone by analysis, she was able to remember, with great sorrow, and a pleasure beyond words, the feel of her mother's coat against her cheek as a child. Around this fragment she will have to construct a less prosperous, less hyperbolic self. The ending of *Hotel Terminus* is, I am inclined to say, like the ending of Winnicott's case history, sentimental, but I am inclined to say that, and preserve my dignity, only because I often do not hold to the wisdom of foolishness, but to the Kolb-like worldliness of corrosive sophistication, soured idealism become irony. The foolish truth of my response was that I found the film's conclusion almost unbearably moving. At the end of Ophüls's film we meet the woman who cared for the Jewish children of Izieux—a spot on the continent, she calls it—children who were deported by Barbie to be murdered in the camps. The children, she says, knew that their parents had already been deported, and we see a photo of the wan face of Meyer Bulkha, a little boy depressed by the world he must inhabit, as Ophüls here almost dares us to feel sentimental towards this past, dares us (in J. D. Salinger's brilliant definition of sentimentality) "to love the world more than God does." We see the countryside of Izieux, the snow melting, water dripping from the eaves, and hear a letter of one of the children, a young woman. She speaks of the beauty of the snow. She thanks her parents for sending clogs. "Now my feet will be warm. . . . The snow is melting." We see the countryside from a window. "Soon Spring will be here.

I will never forget what the South is like." She thanks her parents for a blue checkered shirt. . . . Only the victims can speak, and perhaps only the dead can, if we have been sufficiently harrowed, if we have acknowledged the bitter emptiness of our unreal present, return a few bits of the world to us (clogs, snow, a checkered shirt).

It is hard (because so foolish) to speak of my mingled feelings of pain and relief when those few objects were handed to me. I have spoken previously of the cost of remembering, as it is embodied in *Shoah,* and perhaps in Jewish ritual, how the constant remembering of the dead can obliterate the present. But there are, apparently, gifts given by the dead as well, the utterly powerless, infinitely greedy, not always innocent dead. (And how foolish they are as well, so silly as to have died!) Perhaps they can, from time to time, grant us, for our service to them, our costly, pious continuity with their tradition, some small fragments of the world (the ritual candle? a cup of wine?).

In the final moments of the film, Mme Kaddoush, a survivor of Auschwitz, speaks to Ophüls outside the house in Lyon where she and her family had once lived. She remembers that her neighbors had shut their doors as her family was led away. I am almost a proper fool by this time, and know (though I cannot bear) what "home" means: not nothing, and not very much. Ophüls and Mme Kaddoush climb the stairs she had descended with the Nazis, and she speaks of Mme Bontout, who, as the Nazis led her family away, tried to pull the little girl into her apartment. "I feel a fondness for her, not for the others." One of the Germans saw Mme Bontout try to snatch the child from death. He grabbed the girl back, and slapped Mme Bontout so hard she fell backwards. The movie, the voice of Jeanne Moreau says, is dedicated to her, a good neighbor. —Supposing you are so foolish as to think such people might exist!

What D. W. Winnicott, that humane man, wishes for his patients—that they might take their trauma back into the realm of infantile omnipotence—is, I realize now, the impossible, not quite secular, psychoanalytic equivalent of saying Kaddish. Kaddish, the Jewish prayer for the dead, praises God, his justice and his power. One hopes for the survival of the Jewish people, but there is little in the prayer that pleads with God to restore one's loss. One praises God, and death comes from God, even the death of one's beloved, as all things do, even what we call evil. Kaddish is a cure for piousness and sentimentality; through the right worship of God we come to prize the world properly, not to love it more than God does. Can we say Kaddish for the dead of the Holocaust? Can we refuse?

I think sometimes, as many others have before me in remembering these horrors, of the end of the book of Job, where God Himself says Kaddish for Job's family, singing a hymn of praise to His own power, to the pattern, beyond Job's understanding, that makes Job and destroys Job, and could not create him and sustain him if it did not also destroy him. When I spoke of these films helping us take these events back into our infantile omnipotence—reconnecting them with our instinct for survival, but most especially also for destruction and for our own death—I mean that these artists are fitfully trying to reinvent a way to say Kaddish. These events must be inhabited by eros and death, those forces whose struggle makes us. To join oneself to that which wills one's own death, to occupy every position, would be a way of accepting that death is part of the pattern that gives us; to be, in imagination, victim and executioner is to accept, and even to praise, God. But this talk is speculative; perhaps Kaddish cannot be said in this attenuated, secular, immanent way; and I am nauseated when I even imply that there is such a pattern that includes Auschwitz; Bergen-Belsen; Chelmno; Treblinka; Sobibor; Birkenau; Belzec; Buchenwald; Theresienstadt; Dachau. —Yet surely the forces that formed us formed the world, surely history is not simply outside us, something that happens; surely we might, with proper instruction, join the world in mutual reformation? And surely Kaddish, that prayer I cannot yet say, the prayer for the dead, must precede imagining the new dispensation I longed for at the beginning of this essay, a new political (or is it religious?) vision, which does not deny, but will re-vision our use of the death instinct, so that life might continue. —But this essay can only mark my intention to say that prayer; my desire; my as yet repeated failure.

A NOTE ON THE TYPE

The text of this book was set in a typeface called
Times Roman, designed by Stanley Morison (1889–1967) for *The Times*
(London) and first introduced by that newspaper in 1932.
Among typographers and designers of the twentieth
century, Stanley Morison was a strong forming influence—as a
typographical advisor to The Monotype Corporation, as a director
of two distinguished English publishing houses,
and as a writer of sensibility, erudition,
and keen practical sense.

Composed, printed and bound by The Haddon Craftsmen, Inc.
Scranton, Pennsylvania
Designed by Mia Vander Els